GRATITUDE AND ACKNOWLEDGEMENTS

So much credit and gratitude must go to several people that came alongside me and gave birth to this book.

Sharon Horejsi-Conroy was my inspiration to keep going. I made myself accountable to her for what I got done and it worked. Sharon, I cannot thank you enough for being there and being such a great encouragement. Sharon is a dear friend.

Nina Donato came back for lessons and graciously spent hours at the beginning of my editing the text. She sat knitting and listened to me read the book out loud and then would work her magic. Nina made me think, and helped me make the text come alive by her critique and wisdom as an English teacher. I deeply appreciate Nina's generosity of her time. Nina did the beginning but not the final editing.

Anu Gunn has been my student, video director, producer, and photographer. He is my go-to person for all sorts of advice, but mostly and foremost, Anu is my friend in whom I owe much to be thankful for. Anu, you will always be near and dear to my heart.

Darren Hardy, my mentor, has influenced me so much. Because of his "Insane Productivity Modules" I was able to be productive and focused. His mentorship propelled the finishing of this book in record time. Thank you Darren for all that you do to improve people's lives. You have been and continue to be a blessing.

Bree Melero did the final editing with me. I am so fortunate to not only have Bree as my student but also as an editor and marketing person. She is so gifted in all these areas. Bree, thank you for rescuing me with your editing skills. I am so grateful for *you*!

Cousin Marty Devlin, (Little Marty), thank you for so many of the family photos.

I Will Not Grow Weary

Survival and Success
A Singers Guide to Singing

MARQUITA WATERS

Running Song Music and Publishing

Marquita Waters
www.http://MarquitaWater.com

ISBN: 978-0-9980322-0-7

CONTENTS

INTRODUCTION

*Careers bring many highs and lows, but your
steadiness of self will carry you through them all.*

When I was a teen, an agent would call and book you for shows. In those days there were house bands in the venues, and you would bring your music for them to play. It was a variety show, it was a job, and you loved to do it. Mom had been working with these agents as a tap dancer when I started being booked on shows with her. She had friends that did these shows like Ruth Day, a xylophone player, or Nat Ray, a comedian. Sometimes we would pile into a car together and go to these jobs. I just loved to sing, and here I was with all these people that loved what they did. As we drove, I would sit quietly in the back and listen to everyone. I was quiet till it was time to go on stage, then I came alive.

Better Late Than Never

I got to watch some of the acts. The one I have to tell you about is Nat Ray, the comedian. She was a riot on and off stage. Nat came on stage with a form-fitting evening gown. She tore it off to reveal boots and a short dress that flapped in the front. Then she put her hair into 2 long pieces with rubber bands coming up and out to the ends to support them. One went straight up from the top of her head. The other came straight back and out from the back of her head. Nat would say, "Girls, wear your hair like this and no one will bother you." She also sang a song, "Better Late Than Never". You would never forget her act once you saw it. I just had to share that... but why? Those words, "better late than never" stayed with me as time has passed. Not being a teen anymore, I can see how easy it is to let go of your dreams or what you love to do, as I did for a time. It is hard work, and after a time, it may seem too hard. Nat and others were in their forties and were not looking for stardom. They were making a living, but they still loved doing it. They loved being on stage, and you could see it when they came backstage. They were tired and complained when the performance didn't go right. But they were still doing what they *loved*. So does being in our forties, fifties, or even seventies mean we no longer look for stardom? It isn't that we seek stardom but that we continue to look towards being the best we can be. Love what you do and don't stop doing it. Don't hold back for any reason.

Be brave, it is better late than never!

I considered myself on equal standing with "stars." When I was that teen, the news was I was going to make it very soon. I was confident when I was singing. People said they thought I was made of steel as I belted through each song and performing situation. That steel was real on stage but a facade otherwise. As my career moved along, there were private and personal hurdles that took decades to overcome. That's why I will share my life and many struggles that I've experienced: things I have learned, conquered, survived and redeemed. Some are mistakes (boo-boos in life) that have been opportunities to learn from and acquire a measure of wisdom, as well as knowledge. I am passing it forward.

Our voices aren't just coming from a physical standpoint, but very much a mental one. So your wellbeing and enjoyment of what you do is my concern and goal for you. The "how to" is there for the taking and will help you tremendously. Maybe the stories I tell will ignite a desire in you to get over and past hurdles that can hinder or even cripple your success. There is always a silver lining, and our job is to find it, hold on and soar.

Why Did I Decide to Start Teaching Voice?

There was a lot of turmoil in my home, and when I was very young, I would take out my anger by hurting my voice. I would scream inside and try to push and strain. Well, I was successful. I was taken to doctors, and they said I had a broken blood vessel on the vocal folds… not the best news. I can't remember what remedy was given, but when I went back they said that it was as good as it was going to get. From the look on their faces, it seemed the prognosis for my singing future was dim… Hummm. Did I stop hurting my voice then? Weeeell no. It was years later I had to face my habits and do a drastic but greatly expanding change. I found that when you lose or abuse your voice, you can bring it back.

Don't sit in your problem; work it, fix it, use it to go forward - Ah, success!

Voice Therapy

In my mid-twenties, after years of abusing my voice, I was hoarse and went to an ear, nose, and throat (ENT) doctor at the University of Pennsylvania. He examined me and told me I had nodes, which are benign tumors on the free edges of the vocal folds. He walked me down to a voice therapist at Penn, which was not to my liking, as I thought I could handle whatever was wrong… Hmmm! Does this sound like you? Well, the problem was I was ignorant and stubborn. *Joan Geller*, the therapist, saw right through me and realized I wasn't going to listen to very much she said. So she started handing me books to read, as well as explaining what needed to be done in voice therapy.

That was the beginning of my future in teaching. I started reading and listened to what Joan had to say, but still, I was resistant to correcting my pitch which was too low. My voice was raspy and so many people loved that. I wanted to be loved, so changing that wasn't in my plan. I had to decide whether I would keep my voice as it was and continue to have problems, or change and clean up my bad habits. I decided to change. The doctor told me I had to stop singing so the nodes could recede. For eight months I didn't sing and did most of what was required to have the nodes go away. But more than that, I acquired a lot of new information about the voice, as well as confirmation on what I already knew. I decided to start to give that knowledge to others and help them increase their talents, understand and improve their voices, as well as assist with the vocal problems they had. Voice Therapy, which I will go into in more detail in this book, changed how I approached singing and helped me launch a new beginning in teaching.

I know what you are going through when you go for a note and it hurts, or it won't come out. Some of you are like I was, and you think if you lose the rasp (even though you are losing your voice all the time) that you won't be as popular, or you won't like your sound. Think hard on this, as a lot of talented people like Janis Joplin went down very early in their lives. Sure you loved hearing her raspy, straining, suffering voice, but it represented her turmoil. Your voice will take some of this, according to the strength of your muscles, but you do have to respect your muscles and yourself through training and voice therapy.

I decided to write about myself, my mother and my father to set the stage for you. This had a bearing on what transpired with my career and vocal ups and downs, things that taught me everything I know and want to share. All of what I experienced has brought me through to being more of a life coach as well as vocal coach to my students. I have turned the bad to good and use the great stuff to influence and make a difference in peoples' lives as well as my own. So as you get to know me and as I tell you about some of my life as a performer, you won't be disappointed; you may even relate to it.

*Life is an adventure waiting for **you** to unfold.*

PART I

Walking Through The Years

Marquita Waters

*Anu Gunn took this shot when we were shooting the
music video for my original song "Christ".*

I was born June 14th, 1947 at Hahnemann Hospital in Philadelphia, Pennsylvania. My mother took singing lessons when she carried me. I must have been listening intently, and then being named after an old waltz - well, I was destined to warble.

In my beginning years when I was very little, around 5 or 6, we lived with my grandparents in Germantown, Pennsylvania. I don't recall much before that. Mom needed help raising my older sister Suzette and me. Dad was overseas in the army. You see dad and mom were separated at the time.

110 W. Wyneva Street, where we lived, was a row home. All of the row homes had porches that you could see all the way down the block. I loved singing and rocking chairs. I would go out on the porch where there was this wonderful rocking chair and rock and sing like a happy little bird. It seemed the most natural thing to ask the neighbors if they would want me to sing for them. Every entertainer needs an audience you know. And even if they started to say no, I just started singing. I couldn't hear anything because I was focused on singing and didn't wait for the go ahead. I just loved to sing, so I did.

At around seven years old, still living with my grandparents and after being separated for four years, mom and dad got back together. Mom was pregnant with their 3rd child, my sister Melody. We moved to Upper Darby, Pennsylvania for about a year and then to Lansdowne, Pennsylvania, to a single home, which was the family home while all of us were growing up. As I did the dishes in the kitchen in Lansdowne, I would sing my heart out. Mrs. Ciccerelli in the house across the way could hear me and sometimes would wave because her window was just across her driveway. She always said she loved to listen to me sing and was surprised she could hear me from that distance even with the windows closed… Hmmm.

The Japanese maple outside was a great place to wonder about life. It had a Y shape that I could step into and sing as I leaned on the slender but strong branch. Another branch that came out to the side of one of those main ones was where I would climb and sometimes hang upside down. This was my place of escape in our backyard. I wondered about life and sang as I stood or sat, holding on to my wonderful friend. I wonder if you have a special place that you can go or went to, just to be lost in the love of singing or some other art.

Dad and mom slept late so we had to get ourselves off to school. Suzette, the oldest, made breakfast and that was okay except for when she made scrambled eggs. She always burned the butter she cooked them in, yuck!

You were on your own with dressing, and I guess I didn't do such a great job. One day, Sister Seraphine at St. Philomena's Grade School where I attended, called me over where she was surrounded by a group of girls. I knew I was in for it. She usually called you over to bring out some flaw, and I always had a flaw or 2. Sure enough, she was after my hair. She wanted to know who did my hair, and I told her I did. She said she was going to send me to a mother who knew how to do hair. Then Donna Blue, (I will never forget her name) said, "You can send her to my mother." I hated Donna Blue. Sister Seraphine was just being her nasty self. Another time, I was wearing a chain that had many medals on it - really, there were a lot. I don't know why I had so many medals. I think I couldn't choose between them, so I put them all on as I got dressed in the morning. Again, Sister Seraphine called me over, "What's this," she says as she flicks the medals around my neck. I can't remember what I said, but I never did that again.

I was in 8th grade when my sister Melody was in 1st, and Sister Seraphine told me anything she did, I was responsible for. Sure enough, Melody threw up in school, and guess who had to clean it up... Hmmm. No, this isn't about singing, but don't you just love the stories? And if you went to Catholic school years ago you definitely had stories. Sister Seraphine was a pill and a tough one to take. But when she taught you, you knew it inside out.

Do You Want to Be a Model?

Walking home from grade school one day I decided to try to walk like a model. So each step I made carefully, going from toe to heel, toe to heel, toe to heel, etc... etc... etc... It felt weird, but that was how I thought you had to walk. My head was high, and each step was closer to being poised like the models. Suddenly I noticed two boys walking a short distance in back of me. They caught up and said "Hi." They were in the same grade I was. One of them asked me why I was walking so funny. I must have been a nice shade of red as I told them I was practicing walking like a model. They were nice about it, but I knew they thought I was weird. I never did that again. Did something like this happen to you? No worries, you have plenty of company.

Opportunity

It Was the 4th of July. I was wandering around as usual, when I came upon a celebration about a mile away from where I lived. Chic Mullery was the MC (master of ceremonies). He was busy announcing the happenings of the evening. I went up to the side of the raised stage and called to him. Chic came over to me and I asked him if he knew Mary Snyder. He was surprised to be saying he did and that he had done many shows with her, looking at me with a questioning stare. I announced that I was her daughter and that I sang. I can't remember if I asked him or he offered, but that night I sang. I rushed home and couldn't wait for my mom to get home from her show. I was in bed but hardly sleeping. When she came home I sat up and announced that I had been in a show and sang. Mom was so surprised but very pleased. I couldn't have been more than 10 or 11 years old at the time, but I seized the moment through instinct. I didn't ponder over it, I just opened my mouth and there it was. Don't you wish all opportunities flowed like that?

*Marquita 1952 - This was across the street from
110 W. Wyneva Street Philadelphia, Pa.
My eye was swollen from a bee sting,*

Mary Waters

*Dancing was mom's whole life. She was great at it and taught me
staging, presence, and how to be poised as well as ethical. I deeply
admired her tenacity. She was loved by her students as well as me.*

Mom, Mary Snyder, was born Nov. 16, 1919, and was brought
up around Philadelphia, Pennsylvania. She was the youngest of 6,
three girls and three boys. Mom would tell us over and over again
how she walked the hills of Manyunk. You know you never suffer
more than your parents did.

She loved dancing from an early age and studied for many years
with her teacher Pete Conlow, who guided her through tap, ballet,
and acrobatics. She continued dancing into her 70's with teaching
and performing. Earlier mom traveled the country doing shows as a
tap dancer, a single act, and was the fastest spinner I have ever seen.
This is how she met dad for he was a bandleader in the hotel where
she was booked.

When we lived with mom's parents, Nana and Pop Pop, in their row home in Germantown, Pennsylvania, there was my older sister Suzette, mom's sister Aunt Marty, her husband Uncle Al, and their daughter Little Marty (as everyone called her). Suzette and Little Marty were very close; I was the tag along. Life was pretty normal there with Nana and me taking the peas out of the pods, as we watched "Our Miss Brooks," "Amos 'n' Andy," "I Love Lucy," and many other shows. We had a great time together. Pop Pop did stain glass window work and smoked a pipe. His favorite song was "Look for the Silver Lining." We used to dunk ginger snaps in milk together, which was so much fun. (After writing this I went out and bought some ginger snaps to dunk... Mmmm.) As in many homes, maybe yours, there was the obligatory showing of our talents when family came over. I loved it, but Suzette and Little Marty really didn't.

Since mom worked, Aunt Marty helped with the care of us. She hated to comb my hair, and I hated her pulling through it, so after a while I thought I had a solution, or maybe just a little payback. There was a closet under the stairs that everyone ignored except me. I loved to go there where no one else was, to sit alone. I would comb my hair in this little hideaway, relishing the moments to daydream and hum softly. One day, I got the idea to bring a new comb or brush in till I guess I had them all. My aunt went around complaining that she couldn't find any combs or brushes. I would be sitting in my little coupe-hole... laughing. I was finally found out, but it was fun while it lasted.

I loved to bring coffee to mom in the morning. She would be sleeping later than Nana and I because of the shows she did at night, and also because mom loved her sleep. We, nana and I, would be busy and all of a sudden hear her tap a shoe on the floor to indicate she was up and bring her coffee. I insisted on taking it up to her, but mostly so I could sip just a little off the top... a sip here, then a sip there, checking to make sure the cup still looked full, as I slowly made my way up the stairs. No one ever suspected; my love of coffee has never ceased, and I still use evaporated milk as mom did.

It was in the middle of 3rd grade in Germantown when one day mom announced she was going back with dad. I pleaded with her not to. I even picked up a chair and said, "I'm strong, you see mom, I can take care of you." Why was I so against them getting back together? You will understand as we go along.

I didn't know much about it, but dad and mom were going to have another baby and so we were moving to Upper Darby and then Lansdowne as I mentioned before. I don't remember much about mom in Upper Darby. I just remember roller skating as much as I could and dad making us practice piano. Even though Suzette hated it, she had to also. Dad had a temper and you never knew when he would blow up. As I said, I tried to roller skate - a lot.

Our home in Lansdowne had a very large basement that was the size of the whole first floor. The first floor had a large living room, kitchen with a pantry, and a small back room leading to the backyard. There was the old living room which was turned into a dance/practice room. A sun porch sat on that side of the house next to the old living room. The 2nd floor had three bedrooms and a bathroom. There was a 3rd floor that had two bedrooms and a bathroom. The driveway led to a big garage and backyard where my Japanese maple sat. It lead all the way back and around to the back of the garage where we would burn all the leaves that fell in the fall. There were lilies of the valley that appeared certain times of the year. Ladybugs and butterflies would dance around you. In the driveway I would spend hours catching and releasing those butterflies. They were so beautiful. I got lost in their beauty and just being free and outside with them. We had clovers that gave me four-leaf clovers when I looked in earnest. I was in 4th grade when we moved there.

I would listen to songs on the radio and dance with the refrigerator door. Having a live partner, a guy, was rare so my sister and I invited some of the neighborhood boys over. There was this time when mom went to work, she reminded Suzette and me, as if she knew, not to have any boys in the house (we were teenagers). We waited till mom was securely gone and signaled for them to come into the old living room where we could dance. Well mom doubled back and we saw her come in the driveway. Everyone scattered and was gone by the time she came in, but she knew and warned us not to try it again. I don't think we ever did. You never wanted to cross dad, and mom, well, mom didn't get mad very often but when she did you felt sooo bad. I can remember her hitting me maybe 3 or 4 times in my life. I was always in the wrong when she did, which made me feel absolutely the lowest to get her that mad.

I was a teen when we went on shows together. She was the dancer and I the singer. Yes we drove with other entertainers "acts," but mostly just her and me. She drove through weather not many would dare. There was snow and ice on the road and mom made it through. You couldn't see a thing through the windshield but she plowed on and got us to every job. It was amazing. I would watch and memorize how she did things with the steering and pedals, just in case I had to take over if something happened. I wasn't old enough to have a license, but in an emergency, I was going to be ready.

In the beginning, I was paid $25 a show, and I remember being on so many different ones. We did the VFW halls, Shriner's Clubs, The Log Cabin Inn, Drexelbrook Country Club, and so many other small venues, where they all had house bands, served dinner, and had a show. Once, I remember being sandwiched between 2 strippers. (Yes, you read it right.) I never saw what they did, but I kept thinking oh my gosh, this is weird. And as I came on stage I felt stranger still, wondering why I was booked on that show.

My career kept moving up and the bookings and money went with it. Mom had to accompany me, and I became the focal point and potential star. It must have been hard on her as she still was performing, sometimes on the same show, and had the rest of the family, her practice, and life to deal with as well.

Suzette reluctantly came to some shows early on, but it was short-lived as she wanted no part of show business. She saw what I was going through which didn't help. As soon as she could, she got herself up to the third floor, where no one else usually went, but was a catch-all for odds and ends. Remember there were two bedrooms and a bathroom, so Suzette moved from sharing a bedroom on the 2nd floor with me, to this little hideaway. She went to college and married her high school sweetheart.

Suzette was named after the dish, "Crepes Suzette." Mom had a nickname for all of us: Hers was "Velvet," mine was "Peaches & Cream," Melody was "Angel," and the last daughter Marietta, was "Princess." There was a baby that died at birth and would have been mom and dad's first child. He was "baby boy." I really wished I had a brother. Dad always wanted a boy, and when Marietta was born he didn't even go to the hospital.

I always loved cats and dogs, and mom had a hard time if I saw one in the street after a show. Now she had a way with them also. She nursed many a bird back to health, and when I would arrive with a cat in my arms as I came to visit later, she never said a thing to me. She took several of them in that I had found and gave as presents to my two younger sisters. Both dad and mom never said a word; they just took them in.

I remember one time, a very rare time, dad went to church with us. While walking out and down the street, I saw mom and dad holding hands. All I could think was that they really did love each other.

One time when a priest came to visit us, dad pulled him aside and asked him if he would talk to me about not having to go to church. I sang the night before a lot of the time and needed to sleep. I think mom was fit to be tied. The priest just looked at dad; I don't think he had ever been asked that… another Hmmm.

Mom Taught Us What She Did Best

She (and dad) insisted that straight from school you had to practice then homework. Practice was in the old living room that was set up as a dance studio with mirrors lining the walls and wrought iron bars for ballet that were secured through the hardwood floor. All of this dad had set up for mom. Mom would go through her routines and help us to be poised with ballet, tap and acrobatic lessons. She insisted on us standing up straight which she helped you with every--- single--- day. I hated it then, but I am so grateful because I see so many people look hunched over, unassured, and just plain old bad from not keeping their body erect.

Mom also said you have to hit every corner of the stage and boy do my sweeties/students know I insist on that too. Thanks mom for all you taught me. You are here helping so many be their best.

Many Years After I Left Home

I would talk with mom on the phone. It became apparent how focused she was sometimes. She would start talking about her dancing and her body and then say goodbye… that was it. I would stand there with the receiver in my hands (yes it was a hand held) and stare at it as I thought - just chalk it up to "that's mom."

In the end, mom wanted to live with me which I never understood. Her favorite was Marietta the youngest, and they loved each other. They had an act together when Marietta was younger called "The Marietta's." Suzette always wanted mom to live with her, but mom never wanted to be a regular grandmother and Suzette lead a normal/traditional life. Melody would have wanted her there with her but for some reason she wanted to live with me. Maybe mom remembered the little girl who said she would take care of her. Mom passed in 2008, she is with dad now, holding hands.

Arturo Waters

My manager, agent, and teacher - my dad - was an amazing influence in my life for good and bad. The good was really good and the bad was really bad.

Dad was from San Antonio, Texas, born on May 6, 1912. He was a bandleader when he was in the army. While overseas, he studied piano in Europe. His band continued after he left the military and was called "Arturo and His Gay Caballeros." - Gay meaning happy, just to clarify. He and his band played many hotels, and at one of them, he met mom. She was one of the entertainers that he played for. We lived in Detroit with dad where he owned a music store as well as being a bandleader. After their separation, he came to Philadelphia for mom since her family was there. He still had a band, but as the need diminished, he played with fewer and fewer other musicians, till he finally ended up as a single piano player. Around his 40's he started tuning pianos. He started a Mexican food company called "Pepitos" which took a toll on him as he worked so hard and it succeeded for only a short time.

He was on his own from age 13 when his mother died. He tried to live with his father and stepmom but she didn't want him or his brother, so they left. They were alone, just two young boys. My father was spit at, and one of my sisters told me they didn't eat for a week at one point. How hard it must have been to be so young and have to learn how to survive. He never spoke of those times on the street and what they had to do - he was a survivor. He had struggled and made it through with a family and home in the suburbs of Philly. He wanted to protect us but he never dealt with his problems, demons, the past that made him so hard on us and mentally, physically and sexually abuse me. His anger needed a target, and it was mom a lot of the time, the rest of the family, but mostly me. He was my teacher and manager and wanted me to make it for the family. Unfortunately he had one hurdle - me. You want hard work and diligence taught to you, but a line can be crossed when the person teaching has unsolved issues. You will get mixed results of good and bad.

To his credit though, as bad as he was, that is how good he was. I always admired how he would fix things. If he didn't know how to do it, he would read up and then just do it. He was the one that taught me how to cook different foods for breakfast. Several dishes like Guizado (beef dish) or Arroz con Pollo (rice and chicken) were dishes I made when on the road. He did the shopping and always bought in bulk. So down in the basement, we had plenty of food stored, enough for months if needed. He would hide money down there too, some of which mom found after his death. I am sure having experienced his childhood, he never wanted to go without again.

Giving

Dad would come home from his job in Philly as a single piano player downtown, but he wasn't alone some of the time. He would wake mom up to make meals for poor homeless kids, mostly from Cuba. They would come into the bar where he was playing piano and he would start talking to them in Spanish. It must have brought up many feelings in him of his struggle on the streets of San Antonio as a boy. We would wake up from all the noise in those evenings, and as we watched what he did for these boys, well it was something to be admired. We were taught to give and be caring as we watched two very tired parents. They gave of their time, and I am sure money, to care for a young stranger. The boys would leave in the morning, and I am sure, must have felt a little more loved as they went on their way.

Dad had no one to speak Spanish with, as Philadelphia had almost Zero population of Mexicans. He didn't speak Spanish at home because mom didn't speak Spanish. He taught me how to pronounce and sing several Spanish songs.

Dad never talked much about himself or his family, but for me, there were a few things that stood out. He loved his Aunt Marie, his mom's sister. She was this short sweet little woman, whom dad never wanted to disappoint. Aunt Marie was the only family on dad's side that we knew, and we loved her. She lived in San Antonio, Texas and only visited a few times.

Dad's father, our grandfather, Pedro Araiza left the family and started another. Dad's mother was bitter, so she had dad carry her maiden name, "Waters." He had experienced prejudice and didn't want us to go through the same so he kept "Waters" as our last name. One daughter, Melody has changed her name back to "Araiza."

Dad needed to vent his anger, especially when he came home from a job playing piano and singing. Customers would buy dad drinks which made things worse cause then he would fight with mom. She was hit and fell down the stairs several times. When I was an older teen, I had enough of his hitting mom and shouted at him to hit me - which he did.

When I left home, he was the one that told mom to tell me to come home. You see I left at 19 to go to New York. After that, there was a blow-up between Melody, daughter #3, and my dad. He was going to hurt her and she clawed his face. Mom was so scared that she sent Melody away to Uncle George's, mom's brother. Melody spilled the beans about dad. No one knew what went on in our home, as is the case in many abusive homes. Uncle George called dad. Now dad admired Uncle George. He was in the marines and a wonderful man to look up to, as dad did. It was a man he admired telling him he had to change, and mom got brave and told him she would leave also - dad changed. Melody came home and as time passed there was a real relationship between them. Melody would talk with him, and he got real with her. She told me of many times when she would play the violin for him. He listened patiently even though she said the notes weren't exactly perfect, if you know what I mean. There was, for the first time, a real bond with one of his daughters.

Dad taught me things you would take decades to learn. His way of singing the song changed the melody and smoothed out the phrasing. Someone said that I could never sing the melody of the song as it was written. She was mostly right, but that was because dad taught me how to paraphrase the song and make it my own. This is what I pass on to my students, a valued lesson.

He would have me come to where he was playing solo piano in Philly and tell me to sing without the mic, or just take it out of my hands. When your father tells you to do something you want to make him proud in front of all those people, so I did. He knew that would impress them and dad's tips would roll in. Then, when

I did shows, I would begin by coming from the back through the audience, holding a note till I got to the mic on stage. A few times I barely made it but mostly it was easy enough to do, and the audiences loved it. It was a great challenge to meet.

I remember a time when he called mom and wanted me at the club/bar. A popular singer known for holding notes, especially in his hit song was there. Dad challenged him to hold a note longer than I could. Oh my gosh, I was so scared that this man would win, and I would embarrass my dad. I just went for it and kept thinking, "Don't stop, don't stop." He finally gave in. Boy was I glad, and dad was so proud.

Sometimes you can surprise yourself with what you can do. Have you challenged yourself lately? Well, it's time!

Auditions

As a young teen, auditioning was a private appointment, not the cattle call that it is today for "America's Got Talent" or "The Voice," for example. But then again I was with the biggest agency, "The William Morris Agency," and Lee Salomon was my agent. He was the head of the East Coast Office.

When I auditioned I knew the songs so well that you could wake me in the middle of the night, I could get up and sing those songs perfectly. Any song I learned had to be practiced over and over again many times. That prepared me for every audition being a success. My dad played for me on each and they always went great. My confidence was unyielding and my focus was right on the mark. For me though, I couldn't wait to get through each audition, because then came the ice cream! I so enjoyed getting ice cream after. That was my special treat for nailing it, and I always did. I will teach you how to present yourself and give you skills to help you nail it on your audition.

I auditioned for Quincy Jones when he was an A&R man for Mercury Records. He had a top artist agent with him, Joe Glaser. We were in a tiny room and I began to sing as my father played. They were definitely taken back in a good way. Joe Glaser looked at Quincy and said, "She's a thousand years old." Mercury Records wanted to sign me, and I would work with Quincy Jones. But they wouldn't put any money behind me, so my father didn't sign the contract... Hmmm.

Many would say my father was wrong here, but you don't know. If no promotion is put behind you, then you could sit on a shelf, in a manner of speaking. You would not be able to sign with a company that would promote you and this could be for years. You just have to accept the judgment call. Then again if (my father) took a chance and had me work with someone like Quincy Jones, who is a legend in the music field now, it may have turned out great. We will never know but that is spilt milk and not to be pondered on.

An example of taking that leap is Elvis Presley. He gave 50% to a man, Colonel Tom Parker, who managed him to success. Not many of us would give that much and take that big of a chance, but Elvis did. You will have to ponder long on your decisions of who will manage you, if you want a manager. Go slow and see what others say about that person. You are hiring them. Yes, they will handle things but before they do, make sure you have checked them out and they have the same values and goals as you.

Have you had a teacher, manager, agent or family member who pushed you? Your attitude towards them is going to be a factor in the equation. You have to decide to get the good and deal with the bad. They can't make all the decisions, but you have to listen as they may be right. Listen, then you decide. I never had a chance to decide. My decisions were made for me, and that was a major handicap but not now. This has to be your dream, and you must steer the ship. Sure the teacher, manager, agent or family member is there to help but you have to want it. Otherwise, you may get lost in their desires and direction. Decide to lead. It is your career and success at stake. **You** make it happen!

Dad, I could never repay you for all the teaching you gave me. All the hours of work put in to move my career forward. You were hard on me, your anger and the problems you never dealt with did do damage, but I have reaped from the good that you sowed as well, and in that, I thank you, Dad.

ARTURO
And His GAY CABALLEROS

Personal Management
DELBRIDGE and GORRELL
ORCHESTRAS & ENTERTAINMENT
301 Fox Theatre Bldg.   Detroit.

The Casting Couch and Other Stories

Abuse

It has always been known that the casting couch existed. Many were taken advantage of because they were scared of what might happen if they didn't give in, were too naïve, or with some, they would do anything to make it. You must be careful at every turn and station in life as abuse can happen when you least expect it. I share these stories so that parents will guard their children to make sure the teacher, coach, audition, or whatever setting, is safe for them. If you are older, then use wisdom. Be as healthy personally as possible. Abusers will prey on the weak and unexpecting especially. Do not let your child go to a private lesson alone. Go with them unless and until you are sure the teacher is trustworthy. I insist on parents being at least at the first lesson, so they know who I am and what I teach. I have the students record their lessons for retention, but also the parent can know what is happening if they listen to the recordings. When you get older, you will have to assert yourself in certain situations and refuse advances, as they will come. Not only will they come from the industry, but every walk of life, even family as I experienced with my dad.

I remember the men who worked for Mr. Ciccerelli who lived next door and did construction. A small group of them were sitting together on the side of the house in the driveway next to our home. One of them called me over to say that my dress was pretty and to come closer. I did, and he started to fondle me. I pulled away startled. They laughed as I went away. I couldn't have been more than 7 or 8.

I used to walk alone, a little less than a mile to grade school. I would stop by a creek just about every day and talk to God. I threw pebbles in the stream and went on talking to Him trying to grasp and understand life. On the way to school one day, I met a couple coming out of their home. They started to walk part of the way with me for over a year. Since it was quite a while that they joined me to walk, I thought they were very nice. One day they invited me in for some cookies and milk. I was reluctant, but after insisting I went inside. The wife went out of the room and the husband was sitting across from me. He wanted me to come over and sit on his lap. I didn't want to, but he insisted. Since I trusted him, I did. He fondled me. I got up and left. I took a different route to school after that. Can't remember how old I was, but maybe 8 or 9. I never told anyone about both incidents.

I had singing lessons in Philadelphia but in my early teens my parents also drove all the way to New York, about 200 miles, to give me lessons. I had this teacher there for several months when in one lesson he fondled me as we sat on the bench. I told my father and the lessons stopped.

I got out of these circumstances, but all I could think of was why did I have this happen? Why did it happen to me? My first editor, Nina Donato, brought up the fact that I got out of those situations and that I was a survivor. She saw my strength when I only saw weakness, which is how we look at ourselves a lot of the time. It was like I had a mark on me that said, "She can be abused." What is sensed is the vulnerability. If this sounds like you, please open up about it, and get counseling to strengthen **your** self-worth.

Being Able to Refuse Advances at Any Age

I was invited to the Playboy Mansion by Bill Cosby and realized he wanted to set up another girl and myself with a duo playing at the Playboy Club. I said I needed to go home and left the Mansion (I dodged that bullet).

A singer who had several hit songs and was known for his mellow low tones made advances towards me. I had to refuse them very vigorously. Don't be afraid to stand up for yourself no matter who it is.

A well-known Jazz group had a hit song with a female singer in the 70's. Their song made #3 on the charts, so they were looking for another singer and hopefully another hit song. The piano player in this Jazz group heard a recording of me and wanted me to start working on originals and hopefully have another hit song for the group. The manager wanted to meet and talk in his office before my going into the adjacent studio to practice with the piano player. I thought he wanted to know a little about me and would mostly talk about the Jazz group, their plans, and hopes for another hit song. He asked me questions about my life and then told me how bad I was. He threw in other harmful things which left me speechless. What was happening? Why was he doing this? It was an hour and a half later when he finally stopped to let me go into the studio to work with the piano player. My mind was spinning with questions and confusion. Was I really bad; what did I do wrong? I went into the studio to start working on the group's song with the piano player. This was a well-known musician and leader of the group. He was expecting to hear the same sound he loved on the recording. Instead, my voice was as small as I felt. He asked me if the key was right. It wasn't, but I said "Sure." I had been belittled and berated. It was like my self-worth was gone, and I was just a shell standing there. The session ended and he was polite, but you could see he was disappointed – so was I.

At the second rehearsal session, the manager wanted to speak to me again before going into the studio. It happened again. This was crazy. Why wasn't I able to speak up? I knew from my childhood that I was vulnerable and needed help. I had started counseling a short while before this. I was reading self-help books, and one was on boundaries. All week long before the third and what was to be the final session, I prepared to stand up for myself. I prayed for inner strength and visualized a wall between him and me. That way I felt he couldn't get to me. I could get paid and leave. It was a great opportunity that turned out to be a psychological nightmare.

Sure enough, he started, and I started visualizing. I got the strength to say I needed to get to the studio and start the session. He tried to stop me but I kept going. The door was always locked after I was in and I knew I had to make it passed that door and into safety. I was there shaking, but he was on the other side. He was banging on the door saying I was to go and not get paid. The piano player was calm as I told him I just wanted to be paid scale for the three rehearsal sessions. The manager was banging on the door, but the piano player was calm? Did this happen to other women? This was horrible, and I was getting out of there. The piano player made sure I got paid and I never saw them again.

Think of all the others who have gone through much more demeaning things than this. Think of the stars that are hooked on drugs or that have committed suicide. They needed help, counseling, and care for their personal as well as their professional side. If you have had any traumas as I had, and haven't gotten help, then be aware that there are people who will sense it and use it. Protect yourself. If you have any suspicion that things will go badly, or you won't be able to speak up for yourself - bring someone with you. Don't go it alone. You can have someone call you if you suspect a problem at a meeting. Protect yourself and follow your gut. It will tell you when something is fishy.

My Teen Years Into My 20's

Teachers In My Teens

There were teachers in New York like Marty Lawrence who was great. Mr. Lawrence would just do vocal exercises for the whole lesson. I still use an exercise he did and share it with my students. Good teachers are hard to come by, but they are out there, so find one. Don't accept anything but the best.

Teachers from the Academy of Vocal Arts in Philadelphia, like Dorothy Di Scala, gave me operatic training. She felt I was ruining her training with the "other singing" I was doing which was belting. Maybe she didn't realize that she was giving my voice the muscular balance it needed. Still I learned and loved singing the Ariettas she taught me.

I asked questions about breathing with another teacher at the Academy. He just kept saying. "Oh, you're doing it right." He knew a method but not why it worked, or didn't want to share why. He didn't last very long. In fact, most only lasted a few months as I learned all they had to give in that amount of time. Most didn't challenge me and a good teacher must, it is crucial.

My Parents - Discipline and Learning

Did you watch "Back to the Future?" In one of the scenes, Marty McFly was transported back to the days when there were soda fountains. Just down the street from where we lived in Lansdowne there was a drugstore that didn't have booths but did have a soda fountain. Dad didn't allow sodas in the home so every once in a while we could go to the drugstore, sit at the counter and order a soda. I always ordered a cherry coke or a root beer float. When I would come home from high school, I would pass the neighborhood kids. They would be hanging out in front of the drug store. I could stop and talk but not for long because I had to get home. Was it to do homework? No, it was to practice! There was ballet, acrobatics, and tap for mom; then there was piano and singing for dad. After I did those of the highest priority, then came homework. There was no hanging out as I wished I could do with the neighborhood kids, and to this day when someone says "hang out" I say to myself, what is that? I don't hang out and now don't want to. If you are serious about your goals, you will resist "hanging out" also. Another no-no was having the T.V. on during the day. Again, to this day you will not find the T.V. on unless it is the weekend or a special show on at night. Now I'm grateful for having learned such helpful habits. If you are going to be really good, no great, you have to work hard and be disciplined to spend your time wisely, and that means a lot of practice.

The Hoffman's owned a deli down the street on the same side and block as the drugstore. I would go there to learn my Jewish songs like "Havah Nagilah," "Wus Geven Is Geven Un Nitu," and "Yosell Yosell." When business died down, Mrs. Hoffman would sit with me and teach the proper pronunciation of each song. When I played the Catskills in upper New York, the audience was impressed with how well I sang but also how well I pronounced the words of the song. People that help you along the way like Mrs. Hoffman are never forgotten.

In the mornings we had to be quiet, especially on the weekends when mom had shows and dad had to play piano. We answered the phone professionally, like we were the secretaries getting names and numbers. We let whoever called know we would give them the message that they called. You would run to the phone to make sure it didn't ring too many times and wake them up, but also you never knew if it was for you. We were taught to be courteous, respectful and businesslike.

Dating

If I dated, it was over after the 2nd date. I found out just recently that dad told one boyfriend, who was around too long, that I was going somewhere and didn't have time for boyfriends. I also found out the guys in the neighborhood called me the blessed virgin because I never dated or wouldn't even kiss in my early teens.

I tried to have friends, but when your home life has outbreaks of anger, and you don't know when they will occur, you tend to shy away from having anyone over. The one and only time I did, was when this friend came over and we went to the drugstore at the corner to look at all the different cards. We were having such a great time. All of a sudden, my dad came in and dragged me outside and down the street to the front lawn where he started hitting me. I didn't tell him that we were going to the drugstore was the reason; I lost my friend that day. Most days, even before this I would walk around trying to get lost but always found my way home… Hmmm

On one of the jobs my father did, I met the son of the bartender. He started coming around in his car as I was walking home from school. I was naïve and wanted to be loved. We talked and kissed and I was going to run away with him, so I thought. I was 17 and did run away, but the police brought me back. The boy was nowhere to be found as my father had talked to his father. At the police station I was frantic and told them that my father hit me, and I couldn't go back. They said if I didn't want to go home my only other option was to be put in a home for girls since I was a minor. They promised me he wouldn't hit me anymore and mom kept trying to talk me into coming home, so home I went. After that, I didn't speak very much. I was driven to and from jobs. I was back home, in a prison of sorts. I tried to sleep as much and as late as I could.

Career Highs and Lows

At this time in my life, I was doing great professionally. Working from age 11 to 17, I was getting better-paying jobs and had lots of write-ups in the paper predicting my success very shortly. I appeared in Atlantic City at the 500 Club many times and the owner, Mr. Paul (Skinny) D'Amato became very interested in helping my career. He even renamed me, Mia Morrell, because Frank Sinatra and Mia Farrow were an item at the time. I liked the name and used it for many years. The 500 Club was a favorite spot for the Rat Pack (Frank Sinatra and friends), but they were never there when I performed. Someone who did come in because of Mr. Skinny was a part of the Zanuck movie family. They talked of some grooming changes, but I never heard about what happened with this opportunity. Many opportunities will come your way but there are few that come through. Another that did was a 3 year contract with The William Morris Agency and recordings with ABC Records like "I Have A Mind Of My Own."

My love of singing and how my career was heading couldn't overpower the personal turmoil going on inside. Deep inside my lack of confidence, lack of knowing who I was, and trying to survive only left me groping at life emotionally. Unfortunately, my appearance at The Copa in New York suffered and so did my career because of this.

The Copa was the premier place to play in New York and it was an honor to be on that stage. I was booked there as the opening act for Joe E. Lewis when I was 17 and still having lots of problems emotionally. I looked really confident, but I was so broken and confused. This should have been an exciting time with lots of focus on another milestone, and how happy I was. Instead, I had just been brought back home after running away, and I was broken, confused, and angry inside. All I could think about was how unhappy I was. I was screaming inside.

As I entered the stage, a comedian was sitting at the front table - right in the center. I recognized him. He was Allan King. As my eyes fell on his face I could see what I thought was his disapproval. It was almost like he wanted me to leave right then and there. I let it throw me off. Not only was I miserable, but now this man hated me. That was all I kept thinking. I couldn't wait to get off the stage. Who knows what he really thought, but I was filled with self doubt, so what I thought took over any other reality. I received a bad review. Lee Salomon who was my agent and the head of the East Coast Office at The William Morris Agency stayed with me, but when I was 19, he gave me over to another agent. A sign that I was being demoted so to speak... Hmmm

Philadelphia to New York

My father didn't hit me after I was brought back from running away at 17. For a year and a half I hardly spoke and slept as late as possible. I dreaded getting up for another day. My father's anger kept building; finally one day he just let me have it. Standing in the hall on the second floor he said I was nothing and never would be without him.

I called a nun that taught me at Prendergast High School. We met and I explained what was happening in my home life. She immediately set up a meeting with a priest at Bonner High School next door. I told my mom about the meeting and she drove me there. The priest was very kind and helpful. Both he and the nun agreed that I needed to leave. I didn't want to leave my sisters or mom, but on the way home my mom broke down. She was crying violently and started asking why I thought she was such a bad mom. She was driving recklessly, driving towards parked cars then pulling away. I felt like dirt. I was heartbroken, and knew then the time had come for me to leave. I was 19. The priest arranged for me to go to New York and stay at the Martha Washington Hotel. He paid for the first week. I told a few people I was leaving and they gave me some money, $150. I had 2 suitcases, one on each arm as I went to leave. My father said, "Where are you going?" I said I was leaving and he said, "We'll see about that." He called the police and an officer came. He said, "This girl is leaving with things that don't belong to her." I told the officer that one suitcase had clothing and the other had music that I needed, and it was mine. The officer told my father there was nothing to do, as I was not a minor and I could leave. I left with that police office right then and there for New York and the Martha Washington.

Alone in the hotel, I knew I had to stay away from any family because I might break down and return home. It wasn't easy; it was so lonely in that small room. Being very naïve about life I know now that God protected me in those first months. I later found out the hotel was full of prostitutes and pimps and who knows what else.

The jobs with The William Morris Agency were sporadic, so I needed to get a temporary job as my money was running out. I was good at bookkeeping thanks to my teacher, Sister Seraphine, remember her? I got 100% right on their test. They said no one had ever gotten 100% correct. I was put to work right away and it lasted till I had to travel for singing jobs.

Still with The William Morris Agency and just having gotten managers other than my father, I let them know I had left home and was in New York. The jobs I did were in different states, and I traveled - always alone. My managers handled my money and I was given a small amount to live on. It was very little and to supplement I waitressed. While a customer wanted to order, I was looking at myself on The Merv Griffin Show. He tried to get my attention and I said, "Shhh, that's me," pointing to the TV. He was surprised and started watching too - then I took his order... Hmmm

You Have to Have a Goal

Be a decision maker in your life.

If you are putting a team together, which I didn't realize then, but know now, you must make sure they are on the same page as you. They must have the same goal as you, and you must have a goal. My agent didn't like my managers and that was part of the reason he let me go. The managers were all wrong for me but I was signed to them for 3 years. Having your personal life in order, and knowing where you want to go with your professional life will make or break you. I am there now and share this with you, my students, and others that need my advice.

Drifting Through an Important Time

These were very lost times indeed as my father handled all the business and decisions in my formative years. I was lost when I went on my own at 19. I knew about singing, but that was about it. Pushing for my career or what direction or goals I had wasn't even a thought. This was when Lee Salamon moved me to another agent at William Morris. I wandered through life then, just doing shows where ever I was booked. Being put in the Playboy circuit was a dead end, and there I was. When booked at the Playboy clubs I would be in one city at a time for 2 weeks where I'd put a sign up looking for a room, and stay with one of the bunnies (Playboy Clubs name for waitresses). After making friends and putting on a dinner for all I met, and as the band really got tight with my music, I had to leave.

Traveling with no goals, I just drifted through. Working in and of itself is great but won't get you anywhere. You have to have goals and work toward them. I can't express enough for you to know who you are. That will help you enormously in knowing where you are going.

I played with many acts like Little Anthony and the Imperials, Mel Torme, Jackie Carter, George Jessel, Frankie Avalon, and many more. When I worked with Rodney Dangerfield at the Cherry Hill Inn in New Jersey, he was the opening act and I closed. The next time we worked together he had moved forward - I was his opening act - he closed. Rodney was a very nice person as well as talented.

One final place that I worked for The William Morris Agency was the Chateau Laurier in Ottawa, Canada. It was a beautiful place. I ate the finest of foods from the chef. As I was going on stage from the back of the room one night, the bass player had the intro; he was a ¼ tone off. I looked at the horn players. We just shrugged our shoulders as I was coming in with them, and it wasn't going to be pretty. By the end of the usual time I spent at each place as well as this one, which was 2 weeks, the music was always great. But I was leaving. It was musically very depressing because it took till then to make it great. I wanted more. Also, I was still singing swing which I loved, but as the Beatles had emerged and revolutionized the direction of music, I wanted to sing what I heard. Again, I wanted more. Many musicians didn't like and were unable to make the adjustment to this change in music, which really could have been an asset for them. On the other hand, I embraced it.

I met George Durst who owned a club across from the Montreal Playboy Club where I was booked. He had invited me to visit, so after the Chateau Laurier, I did. There was a group from England playing there. George introduced me to Liz Christian the singer, and we became instant friends. George wanted me to play at his club which I did and with Liz and her band. My contract with the managers was finished, so George signed both of us to a contract. We went to England, got another band and played at George's club for months. This change of music for me, as we did R&B (Rhythm and Blues) was needed, and I loved it. Liz and I were great pals, both around 20 years old. I will never forget our time together, and our egg fight, the most fun I ever had.

Egg Fight

After finishing a gig one night we were going to make breakfast for the band and some girls that tagged along. We were at the refrigerator, Liz and I, and Liz says, "I wonder how you would look with eggs on your head?" I said, "Don't do it, Liz." Of course, she couldn't resist and there went 2 eggs. I said, "You know what this means now don't you?" With that we started throwing eggs at each other, laughing as hard as we could. It was the greatest! The rest of the band began to hear the commotion and came in, only to find an egg coming at them. I was a taskmaster to them; they really wanted to get me. I started down the hall. The drummer picked up a box and threw it. It was powder and it was everywhere. The girls were indignant and left. We were just trying to get traction to get away from whoever was after us with an egg. We finally ran out of eggs and steam. A friend came by to take us to a swimming pool, where we jumped in clothes and all. Cleaning up wasn't as much fun but it was worth it. Liz fell asleep… Hmmm. After decades Liz and I have renewed our friendship, and she came from England to visit with her partner Nicolette just recently. They are a blast!

Even with me wandering through this time, there is always something that you learn. It may have taken me a long time to learn it, but I look back and use this time to show others, to show you, how important it is to have goals. Have fun, but keep your eye on what you want. Know what you want so you are aiming and not drifting.

My 20's

As you walk through life and your career, you will have times when your personal life will have to take center stage. Your family may need you. Take the time to be there for them. It is not always about a career; it is about balance and life is always trying to throw you off.

I left Montreal and had tried to get back with a boyfriend in Seattle, but that was a disaster. So L.A. was the plan, and to start over when I got a call from my mom. My father was dying. He was only 51and had cancer. My Uncle George got a plane ticket for me. I returned to Philly. It would be 7 years before I finally did get to L.A., at the end of 1978, and was right after I started teaching voice.

After I first left home at 19, it was 6 months before I tried to come back to visit. My visits were very sporadic and only lasted a few days before I had to leave. Just a few days and I would start to shake being in the same room with my father; so going back wasn't the easiest decision to make.

I went to see him at the hospital one time after coming home. He said, "I guess it's just about being happy." I nodded saying, "Yeah." He made amends with a lot of the relatives, but he never said anything more to me. At a certain point, you realize that you have to face what has happened and work it through yourself. Even if the person who has hurt you doesn't apologize, you get healthy.

Dad had died (1971), and mom couldn't handle the home in Lansdowne. She didn't want the burden. Again I told mom I would take care of things and sell the house as she was upset and crying. Dad had taken care of the bills, and the checkbook. He was indeed the head of the family, and without him there, she was overwhelmed. I said I would take daddy's part. I had a huge garage sale of several decades of things. From the 3rd floor down to the basement, dad's tools in the garage, all the memories, all had to go to make the mortgage. There was so much to do that I had to move in with my cats to take care of it all. This left the cleaning and sale of the house without a realtor to save mom as much money as possible. Little did I know that when my older sister visited, mom cried to her, so she brought a realtor in who said I had to leave, which I did. This was when I had gone to the ear, nose, and throat doctor and was supposed to be resting as I had nodes (benign tumors). Mom did have her shortcomings. Still, it was the right thing to do to be there and help out, painful as it was.

Life has a way of throwing you a curve when you least expect it, so be ready for the incoming. You may not be able to follow your dream right this moment, but don't lose heart. There is always a tomorrow. If you don't lose sight of it, you will do what you are called and meant to do. In my 20's I had a detour, but as I look back, I had a lot to deal with. I wasn't ready.

Mistakes are opportunities

Keep going, make a new beginning. Just as a new day rises with the sun, so we have a renewed opportunity to right our wrong. Start anew. Don't ponder on what has been but move towards what can be.

Setbacks and mistakes are opportunities for growth and learning. If you are discouraged about them, know that they can teach you to be stronger and work harder toward achieving your goal. If allowed, these can make you a better person. Know that they will come. They are just part of the game. Build new beginnings each day. Let the past be just that, fix it, use it, but don't let it hold you back. Be a winner!

Winning

For years in my 30's but mostly 40's running became my first love. It was something I was good at. At the end of the race you could see a tangible result. Did I win the race? No, but from the beginning in each and every race, I win 1st, 2nd, or 3rd place in my age group. Did I *want* to race? No, because it would put me to the test, and I was used to avoiding that. My coach insisted. He wanted me to start racing, and I was pleasantly surprised. I was a winner. God used running to show me that I did finish things, and I could succeed. What will you use to convince yourself that you can succeed in your endeavors? If you have convinced yourself that you are a loser, or more softly put - you can't win... *you* need a change.

Try – no - DO! Don't just try to do something and give yourself an out. You have to be determined to do it. This applies to your voice but also to your life. Do that audition, go after that note, write that song, do it. In this next story, I broke my pattern and did it. It strengthened me in all areas of my life. What about you?

In Grade School there was a position open for the track team. I wanted to do something other than singing. There was one position left. Another girl and I were going for it. We started to run. My brain was running its own race. "Why are you even trying, you know you will fail, give up." I believed this and didn't even fight. I just let her win. I never even told anyone that I tried out. It wasn't show business so it wouldn't have mattered.

Before leaving Pennsylvania, I started running. I wanted to get in shape but instead, I fell in love. I was running each day at a track. One day I ran 15 miles. I was thrilled. Moving to L.A. and having such great weather I wanted to expand my running. I met a Chiropractor, Dr. King Rollins who soon became my coach.

Running became a passion. It was great therapy, and along with some counseling, I was facing my fears. King wanted me to enter races which I was avoiding. Finally I gave in. Close to the end of one race, there was another woman in my age bracket who was used to winning. A man was running with her and saw me behind them. He turned to her and said, "Oh, don't worry about her; she's nothing to worry about." He said I was no threat to her, and yes, I was going to just let her win. How did he know? Suddenly I remembered my childhood. How I didn't even try to win. I got mad and really upset inside. I was repeating the scenario again - after all these years! Was I still playing a loser's game on myself? No! I decided to try. What did I have to lose? How dare he cross me off as nothing. I had learned that I was something. I needed to seize that moment no matter what.

So I decided to try. In moments I started to gain speed. I was the little engine that could. The man looked back again, but this time he wasn't so confident. I was determined. As I passed her I changed my course from poor little me to I can, and I did! In subsequent races we would see each other. In one she told her running partners, "She's the one you have to beat" - they never did ... Smiling Hmmm.

What is your fear and are you willing to work on it? It isn't easy, but little by little you can break it down, instead of letting it break you. If it is the path you are meant to be on then never give up.

Restrictions and Limitations

How are you restricting yourself and your talents? The tapes we run in our minds often tell us what we believe to be the truth about ourselves, but are anything but that. "Take every thought captive," is what scripture tells us. That is what we

> *How are you restricting yourself and your talents?*

have to do to make valid decisions on what comes to mind. This sound advice will help you to fight for what is really true about yourself and become the best you can be.

Take note of your thoughts, and write them down. So many of us are playing the, "I can't do that," or "that's too difficult" tape. Maybe someone in your past be it an agent, family, teacher, friend or foe, told you you're nothing, or that you can't do something, or that you aren't capable of doing that one thing you love. These are embedded in your brain and replay every time you step up to the plate of life. Now is the time to rewrite the script. Throw the tapes away and replace them. (We don't use tapes anymore anyway.)

The Things People Say Affect Us

I didn't believe in myself or feel worthy in the least. I was told I was nothing and that I would never be anything. I was always losing my voice. My father said that would continue - without him. One day as my father was berating me trying to maintain his hold, I fell to the ground. There I was, nothing, not even feeling human. I began to groan and crawled into my bedroom. My sister Suzette got me up but the damage had been done. For so many years I lived this assessment out with not trying to be anything, too scared to step up to the plate of life to even try. Oh I looked confident, and kept up a good front so no one would suspect how lost and broken I really was.

For a long time I was angry and confused. I started to feel sorry for myself. This is the worst thing you can do. I played the victim and it wasn't fun, but it was safe. It took many years before I finally got help and I did it reluctantly. I went to counseling for a long time, years, because I knew this was what I needed to heal. I am so grateful that I gave in to God and got inner healing for my pain. If you don't face and fix your problems, even though you have been harmed and hurt through no fault of your own, you carry these problems with you. You give them to others, as well as keep yourself captive by the contamination that it causes. This is why my father was full of anger. He never dealt with his demons. Not trying and letting my life fall apart was directly associated with what happened to me through childhood. It needed to be healed and it was - thank God... truly.

Until you face the fact that you are scared or have personal issues that need to be dealt with, they will control you. People may wonder why you aren't using your talent or haven't "made it." They see your talent, and you know you have this gift but aren't using it. Maybe you aren't going for it or trying to make a name for yourself. You will regret it for the rest of your life. Is it easy? Of course not. It took me decades. But is it worth it? You bet it is. I had to take a bulldozer to the monument of fear I built. So pick up your weak areas and kick them till they scream "I am worthy to succeed."

While I went back to Philadelphia and before I had to do voice therapy for nodes on my vocal folds, I played the Wine Cellar in the Sheraton Hotel. There I met a photographer, Tom Keegan. He came in regularly and took many pictures of me. The next picture was taken by Tom Keegan, and to this day I love it and use it. Tom has passed but he remains a fond memory during that time in my life.

KNOWLEDGE, COURAGE, ACTION

Ken Rutkowski gave these 3 insights on his show, *"Business Rockstars,"* necessary for business that I thought were invaluable and they are. I would like to offer my thoughts on them:

Knowledge

When I recall the scripture verse, "My people perish for the lack of knowledge," I know it has such truth for our lives today. We need to gain knowledge on both the personal and professional side. This balances us. I went to counseling to receive help with my own shortcomings. Handling them myself wasn't possible because I didn't know what to do. I also read books and listened to persons who were experts to glean from their wisdom. Gaining this knowledge gave me the tools I needed to understand what was to be done. It helped me win the freedom and strength of character to stand and not withdraw from my life and my career. Knowledge will free you and fortify your skills to face your obstacles.

In this day when technology is moving so fast, we have to do and be much more. We have to adapt to new ways of addressing our careers, be aware of marketing, the social trends, as well as our talents and care of them. There isn't time to waste. If you realize there is an area holding you back, that means you need to address it.

Students come to me and get mad when they can't get a part right or hit a note. I tell them that they are learning how to do it. They are coming to me to get the knowledge *to* know. Don't expect to know something you haven't discovered yet.

Courage

Gain the knowledge you need and then have the courage to face what is holding you back. You need to fight it! It is not enough to establish the fact. It will take working through and past. Now that takes courage.

I told you some of my challenges, and in life - they keep coming. There are and will be many obstacles you will have to face. Don't think you're alone. You aren't. Read, talk, listen and realize that everyone has to face and conquer their own obstacles. Every morning when I get up, I think of what I can be grateful for. Just the fact that I have another day is awesome. Do you have food to eat? Okay, me too. Let's be thankful. List the everyday things that are usually taken for granted and little by little you come to realize how rich you are. Our attitudes help us have the courage to face yet another audition or write that song. Maybe for you it is facing the fact that this is your passion and you need the courage to step up and do it. My attitude changed through counseling. I realized I was part of the problem. It helped me see that I was sabotaging myself with negative and unhealthy habits. Little steps towards a healthy and helpful mindset are what we need. Being grateful brings you into the right frame of mind. I know you can have the courage to move forward and take action towards the desires of your heart. Now you need to *do it*.

⸻ • ❋ • ⸻

Knowledge without action is a cute
ornament to hang on your wall.

⸻ • ❋ • ⸻

Action

I knew I needed inner healing and decided to get help. This was to be just the beginning of a long journey of change. I would come out of some counseling sessions sobbing. Sometimes I was so spent that I could hardly stand. It wasn't easy; it was healing. This is where the rubber meets the road. If there is no action, then all the knowledge you have won't mean anything. Your success personally and professionally will be handicapped as mine was.

One exercise I have my students do in voice therapy is beneficial in working on a negative mindset, which can also be very harmful to your success in any area of your life. First, write down the things that pass through your mind. Take the negative statements and write them down. Yes, write them down. Now, turn each statement around to a positive one. Be realistic with what you write. Go back and reread those positive statements. As the same old negative statements come back around to reinforce their impact, because they inevitably will, you can stop them dead in their tracks with your new mindset. Practice will make the change you need - just believe and start doing.

What action do you need to take? Well, what do you want? If I didn't get up early every morning, this book wouldn't be here. I had to decide to take action. I decided and did. I didn't keep thinking about it. I acted. Now it is *your* turn.

Darren Hardy has just recently reinforced this in me through his "Insane Productivity Mentorship Program." Because of his mentorship I made the book a priority by setting it as an appointment. It was marked on my calendar at a specific time and with no distractions. My phone was silenced. No notifications, no emails. Nothing was allowed to take my attention away from writing the book, my goal.

Taking action on your weaknesses, goals, habits, dreams, or whatever they are, takes a lot of courage and knowledge. You won't be disappointed that you did. You will and should be proud of yourself if you do.

LACC College: 1986-89

I went to college and took all music courses. Piano was a requirement and quite a challenge. I took private lessons from my piano teacher during a break as I was having a tough time. When classes resumed, he wanted to show my progress in the classroom. I was petrified and tried to tell him I couldn't. There I sat getting more and more nervous as he insisted. I started and couldn't control my nerves as my mind kept saying "no, no," "I can't do this." I froze just after a few bars into the piece. He finally let me sit down. I felt so humiliated and knew my teacher was very disappointed. It took many decades before I was able to heal the trauma from my childhood.

This story tells the turning point.

You see:

When I was young, I would sit and look around at the walls and the picture of Saint Teresa hanging above the piano in the sun porch. My father had left, telling me to practice, but shortly, my eyes would start going over this picture. Saint Teresa had such a calm face. A garment flowed around her head and down the sides. She had a cross in her arms that showed Our Lord, rosary beads and roses. It's vague now but then I knew every inch of this picture. The walls that surrounded her picture were made of stone and had cement that held these large pieces of stone together. I would follow the lines between the rocks, look at all the different slight changes they made, and be mesmerized. I was lost in what I saw. Then it was time for my father to come back to see if I knew what he told me to practice on the piano. I quickly went over the piece and got it right. When I didn't, he would start to get mad, yelling and pointing at the page, and then he left to get the strap. He would come back to stretch it out, pulling both ends which sounded a snap to show and intimidate before belting me. I would be dragged by my hair, which was long, from the seat as he was yelling. He had little patience for my wandering mind and was going to beat it out of me. Indeed, as much as I loved my father, I hated him.

Little did he or I know, it is called attention deficit. I needed help focusing. I also had dyslexia, which I later found out. As time passed, I tried to play piano but couldn't put my hands on the keys without shaking. Little by little I put one hand then the other, but still, my attention was next to nothing. It was like I was in prison and had to run away because it was so confining. I tried lessons before and after College, but each teacher couldn't understand that I needed a different way to learn. Because I was accomplished at singing, they couldn't understand my problem and would give me a piece to read and play that was too hard, even though it was a beginner's piece. I couldn't find my place once my eyes left the page, which was often. I was also fired as a student because I couldn't practice and came in with little improvement. I started talking out loud and yelling to encourage myself past the fears of the past and my learning problems. Imagine me sitting there saying, "Okay, okay, you can do this"... "Oohhh" (louder still)... "Come on, let's go!"..."Okay, okay!!"...

I tried to explain to the teachers, but they had a hard time with this breaking through method I was doing. Another teacher asked me if I had thought of taking up guitar... Hmmm. Finally, one teacher let me keep yelling as I got past my fears, memorize the piece, and play it. For the first time in my life I played a piece through and I think I was in my 40's. (Some things take a long time.)

By the way, years later, the guy that fired me as a student bumped into me and apologized. He realized I was trying but had an attention deficit problem and an eye hand coordination problem. Who knew!

I had to leave college because my husband at the time was leaving me so I had to concentrate on paying the bills. There was no furniture in the living room except my P.A. That was the trade we made; I kept the P.A. - he took the furniture. When my mom found out, she sent furniture to me from Philly with my sister Melody who was traveling to L.A. Mom had given me some precious pieces that I still look at and treasure. She knew I didn't have a piano so guess what I got now…. yes, I have that piano that belonged to dad and his congas from when he owned a music store. *My piano* is an old Packard upright. It's an antique, and I love playing it. It is all mine now. The bench is another story; it never survived all the blows to the floor, poor thing. Saint Teresa belongs to my older sister Suzette; it was a prize. I asked her for it and she reminded me of this. I won't be reuniting with Saint Teresa over the Packard, but I can almost see her there looking down at me. I give her the thumbs up now.

Most all of my originals have been
written on the Packard.
Redemption.

Conquer a Step at a Time

I wrote several songs after the breakthrough with playing piano. Now I needed to be able to play and sing them. The opportunity came on a Sunday at the Valley Vineyard Christian Fellowship Service. I was to play and sing one of my originals. It would be the first time I attempted it in front of an audience. As I sat, I was so afraid of making a mistake. I went over and over the song in my mind. My fingers moved on my thighs playing the notes as I waited, trying not to be nervous. It was time for me to perform the song. I went to the piano, focused and was as calm as possible. I sang and played through the song. Then I came to a part - there was the mistake ready to happen. For a split second I paused. The panic, the retreat was starting. And then in my mind I yelled, "**NO**! You are **NOT** going to give in." I knew if I stopped there, I would never play and sing in front of anyone again. It was a split second to decide as those thoughts rolled by. I forced myself past and went all the way to the end. That was a pivotal moment for me.

It has gotten easier and more comfortable as time passes, so my advice to you is don't give up on yourself. Fight through. You will have a moment when you need to get past the impasse you are facing, and you can, you will. If I did it, so can you… Happy Hummm.

I don't write these stories for you to feel sorry for me; some of you have gone through much worse. Each of us has gone through something in our lives that has shaped or changed us. Hopefully in the end we meet the challenge. I got help for my sorrows and pains so that I didn't remain a victim. You are called to make sure you are healthy personally. This will help you to emerge as a healthy professional, a success, maybe even a star. Or you can still emerge a star, but inside be filled with self-pity or a distorted self-worth. With that, you are of no help to others as well as poison to yourself. Remember Janis Joplin and the others that have lost their lives so early in their career from an overdose, or other maladies? They never fixed the personal side, and yes, you can make it, but at what cost? Make it and be healthy, that is the trick. If you have been hurt, get help, get well, and get going.

You Love It - Then Do It!

I loved to sing from very early on. To this day I feel the need to express myself with originals and music videos, as well as shows. It can be so exciting to bring that sound from the depth of you.

Communicating it to others and seeing their expression, hearing the applause... Ah, it is so rewarding. For me it has been a way of life, how about you?

You will need to gather as much strength to live a life in the arts where not everyone makes it. In fact, most don't. It doesn't have to do with how much talent you have. Many factors go into someone making it. You need to know who you are, and have a strong constitution to offset the ups and downs that will come your way.

When I ran, I loved the fact that things were concrete. You ran, you finished and there was the time. You knew whether you won or not and I always came in 1st, 2nd, or 3rd. I got my medal and that was that. Not in show business. That uncertainty can leave you in a quandary, even bitter and resentful if you don't have a solid grounding on who you are. Despite this, we still go for it don't we? So do it because you love it. Enjoy the ride and you may have the success you seek. Surely you will enjoy doing what you love to do and in that is success.

My 30's to 50's

I was frozen. Afraid of succeeding and afraid of failing, so I didn't go after anything. I was told I was nobody without my father, by my father, so I lived that. I was told as he banged on the dashboard coming home from his job, where mom brought me to sing, that I have to eat, sleep, and drink show business. I wanted to have the door open and fall out just to get away. He and mom kept saying that you can't have a family life if you're going to make it in show business. I wanted to be happy and have a private (family) life, but I also wanted show business. This confusion and confused thinking stayed with me for most of my life. I fixed my personal life by getting counseling for the past and owning my responsibility to heal all that happened in my life. But my professional side still lay dormant. All this time I was still teaching others; helping them be their best. I was hiding my talents. I was still living out a resistance to succeed because of what I was told as a child. Subconsciously I felt that if I succeeded, I had to be alone. But I felt as if I was a failure by not having succeeded. My professional life lived in this limbo. I realized what was holding me back - *ME*! I started removing the barricade and owning this part of my life.

A lot of stars work on their professional life, but their personal is a mess as we see time and again. I worked on the personal and realized that I needed to apply myself to succeed in my professional life. Unlike what I was told and lived out, I could have both. With my father driving my career, I would have been pill popping and narcissistic, your basic mess of a person, but a star for sure.

My dad was right in the essence of what he was trying to convey. You really have to work hard at your goals. He knew as I know now, that you have to put your whole focus on what you want to achieve. The problem was that he was forcing it down my throat and tried to beat me into submission.

With the inner healing I received in counseling, I forgave my father. In prayer I saw him give back the parts of me I felt he took as he broke my spirit when I was a teen. I wasn't frozen anymore; I was aware and owning all of my life.

Now

What about now? Well the years the locusts have taken away have been restored. My little girl is fully intact. You wouldn't know my past existed. Many of my students and friends are sitting with their mouths open having read what I have revealed. I am sure there is much more to be said, but I will share just a little more and save the rest for another time. There are a few more stories in the next part though, I couldn't resist.

Now, I teach with the enthusiasm of a teen in love. Because of experiencing a lifetime of singing and performing, I can tell what a student needs as soon as they open their mouths to sing. There have been hundreds if not a thousand students come through my door. That experience gives me insight into what each individual needs and what instruction to give so they get it. I can look at their body language and know what our work will entail.

Many people that have reached my age have given up. The business is tough and unpredictable. On the other hand, many are realizing that there is still life to live after stopping or retreating for years, sometimes decades. They are returning to what they love. So why haven't I given up or left this book unfinished? I don't want to! I cannot! I need to make a difference too - in others lives and continue making a difference in my life. I would love to make a difference in your life. With so much time wasted on pondering and fearing, I am eager to use the time that God will give me going forward to do just that. It also benefits me with feelings of usefulness, being alive and being worthwhile. So after decades of not finishing this book, it is in your hands. I do hope my words ignite in you the ambition to go after your dreams. The book *The Millionaire Messenger by Brendon Burchard* inspired me when he shared his story of surviving a crash and never being the same. He realized he did matter and has gone on to share his story, make a difference in many lives, and make a significant income. What are you going to do?

So many of my students call me a Life Coach and I am honored because I do try to steer them in the path that will make them the best they can be, vocally and in their personal lives as well. The more successful I am at releasing the knowledge and experiences I have, the more lives that can be impacted. Boy do I want that!

Getting older is not the ending but a new chapter. As with any age, it has its challenges. I have chosen to meet them head on - life is still what you make it. I do vocal exercises on the way to the gym, and there I workout as heavy and hard as wisdom allows. In 2006, my swing album was released. There were 12 songs in all; five were my originals. In 2010 I finished writing ten originals. I wrote one a month till they were done in December. Two of these originals have music videos on YouTube with more to come. Sure there will be challenges along the way, as well as setbacks, so let *us* meet them head on.

*I will **not grow weary, how about you?***

ANNIE WATERS
- DAD'S MOM

Nanna + Papa

Mom
2½ yrs.

When I was about 2½

Dad as a baby

DAD · ARTURO WATERS · 8/rs.

DAD + his Brother Marvin

DAD AND I WERE BOTH 5 WHE
WE HAD Pony Ride Pictures.

DAO · ARTURO WATERS · BAND PICTURES

Arthur Waters and his RKO recording orchestra, will open the new Mansion night club, formerly the Pomegranate club on the Bur road Saturday night.

To Mother & Daddy
With my most sincere gratitude
and love for giving me a
profession what happiness
much happiness. I love
you all very much.
May

Mom. Mary Jane Spyden

To Jane
with love
May

My Uncle George —
Mom & Dad

Dad & Mom
on their Honeymoon

Dao "Arturo Waters
Band Pictures

1940's

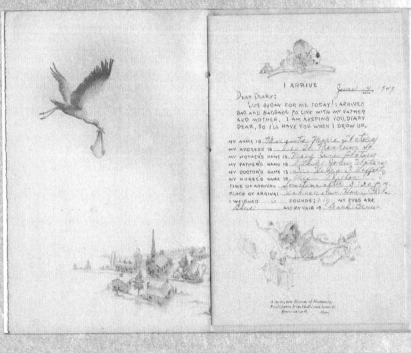

I ARRIVE

Dear Diary:

Life began for me today. I arrived
bag and baggage to live with my father
and mother. I am keeping you, Diary
Dear, so I'll have you when I grow up.

My name is _Marguerita Ingrid _____
My address is _____
My mother's name is _Mary _____
My father's name is _____
My doctor's name is _____
My nurse's name is _____
Time of arrival _____
Place of arrival _____
I weighed _____ pounds; _____ my eyes are
_____ and my hair is _Dark Brown_

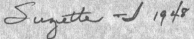

Suzette — 1948

Aunt Marty with Little Marty   1950's

Me + Suzette

Suzette Melody + Me

W146

OCT 1957

1957

Basement of 110 N. Maysvand.

68 W. MARSHALL RD.

1970's it was sold

THIS IS THE
SUNPORCH WHERE
I PRACTICED
PIANO

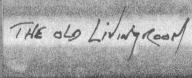

THE OLD LIVINGROOM

S. S. OVER TO B. H.

Did you ever see a dream walking? Well, did you? No? Well, I did.

I saw a dream who not only walks—she sings like the angels and looks like a dish of peach ice cream.

Her name is MIA MORRELL, and when she grows up and I am an old man, I will run away to Majorca. And she will follow me. And we will throw ourselves off a high cliff some stormy night into the wild and wave-tossed Mediterranean. Our bodies will be washed up on the shores of some lonely Greek isle, and young French girls will write poems about us.

In the meantime — to plunge from the lyrical to the literal—Young Miss Morrell, she's only 17, will doubtless have become the biggest female vocalist in show business.

Don't laugh!

These smoke-seared baby blues and calloused ears have seen and heard them from JUDY to ELLA, and this kid already has all the marks of greatness. Remember she's only 17!

It takes a pretty talented thrush to stop them dead at the "Five," and Mia can do it with the flick of an eyelash.

MISS MARVELL
Momma, Mia!

She's back at the 500 Club this weekend after an earlier three-day stint at SKINNY D'AMATO'S saloon last spring. Her voice then was good; today—after getting her high school diploma and losing her tonsils—it is great.

Her voice will get even better with time, but it's her movements, her gestures, the way she can grab and hold an audience . . . BARBRA STREISAND should run away and hide.

And looks? Man, does GETTY have millions? Is there salt in the ocean? Do birds fly?

So, quit your job. Sell your stocks. Break your golf sticks. But go. And see. And listen.

Then join me in Majorca.

You never know what people will say sometimes it is over the top. sometimes false. mostly I took it with a grain of salt

covers that he se...... re more from billboards than he does in person in the Universal color comedy, "The Thrill of It All." The film is at the Roxy Theater.

Someone Got Real Creative With Mom's + My Name

This was my High School Senior Pictures in 1965

Warbling Mia

Mia Morrell is a lovely young thing that can sing like a canary and displays some extraordinary talent in the wonderful new musical revue, "Hollywood or Bust," now thrilling crowds of people at Mangam's Chateau, 7850 Ogden, Lyons. This gal is really going to go places and her presentation by Mrs. Helen Mangam is a step up the ladder of success.

Pheasant Run

Carolyn Jones, motion picture actress and star of the ABC-TV series, "The Addams Family," comes to the stage at Pheasant Run Playhouse, North ave., Rt. 64, St. Charles, in the Chicago area premiere of "Ready When You Are, C.B." The comedy runs at the dinner-theatre now through May 22.

I still had time for homework even though I had shows like these at the Riptide

Can you believe this is Morticia Addams?

THE RONETTES

THRU SUNDAY

LITTLE ANTHONY AND THE IMPERIALS
(WITH THE RONETTES)
CONTINUOUS ENTERTAINMENT

OPENING MONDAY

FISHER AND MARKS
(WITH THE RONETTES)
BAR & TABLE SERVICE

★ PLUS SINGING SENSATION **MARQUITA**
★ THE **LOU CAPP REVUE** FEATURING **DANIEL & DAMON**
★ **GABRIEL AND THE ANGELS**

This Is One Star-Studded Show You Must Not Miss!

COMING SOON
FATS DOMINO
AUG. 27 — LABOR DAY

It's All Happening At The

RIPTIDE CLUB OAK AVENUE

Grossinger's '64

I WORE THIS SAME DRESS
IN A PICTURE OF THE CHOIR
AT PRENDERGAST HIGH SCHOOL

MR. GROSSINGER is the
one with a cigarette
in his mouth.

PHILADELPHIA DAILY NEWS   WEDNESDAY, MAY 18, 1966   39

Jerry Gaghan

Katie to Meet
Fabian's Folks

MEETING THE FOLKS: Fabian flew back from Rome Sunday (where he had been working on AIP's upcoming film "Dr. Goldfoot and his Love Bomb") to return to Atco. The film star-singer will introduce his bride-to-be, starlet Katie Regan to his parents and also make arrangements for the wedding to be held in Jersey in September. . . . Hal Holbrook, whose one-man show "Mark Twain Tonight" is a current Broadway hit, will deliver the commencement address and receive a Doctor of Humane Letters degree at Ursinus College, June 6. . . . David Loeb has sold his Food Trade News to Irv Borowsky, who will add it to his . . . chain of . . . papers. Loeb will continue as editor through the . . . organization. . . . Mia Morrell has been signed by the William Morris office. The deal was set by Paul (Skinny) D'Amato, owner of Atlantic City's 500 Club, where the chirper impressed audiences last summer. Initial move by the agency was to pact Mia with United Artists Records.

. . . TOPICS: Len Gochman, who acted as Robe . . . to . . .

NOW WHO PUTS THEIR HANDS UP LIKE THIS — TOUCH DOWN!

When dad wanted me to get up + sing he would play my theme song "Marguerite"

Mom Marvin Wray + Kat R

For People in Show Business, You Need More Than Talent For a Long Career. You Need A Good Business Sense. Dad Had It And Pepito's Was One of Many

Having A Blast!

Some Shows Are Too Much Fun

JOE DE FEO'S NEWS 'N VIEWS

The ballroom of the Bellevue Stratford Hotel glittered and glistened with beautiful women in swishing gowns, and handsome men in after-six jackets last Saturday night. All for the benefit of South Philadelphia's St. Agnes Hospital, which will be razed and completely rebuilt as "one of the best hospitals in Philadelphia". The announcement came as a surprise statement bearing the official imprimatur of the Catholic hierarchy in this area. The guests, most of them interested in the affairs of the old hospital, were stunningly elated.

But it was a teenage Lansdowne girl who really brightened the night and stole the gala show. Mia Morrell took the stage and sang her heart out to the delight of hundreds of enthralled guests in the colorful, flower - bedecked main ballroom. Mia, who graduated only last June from Archbishop Prendergast High School in Upper Darby as Marquita Waters, was "loaned out" from Don Battles' R.D.A. Club as a charity gesture to the hospital. Backed up by the illustrious Howard Lanin orchestra, Mia opened with the up-tempo "I'm Gonna Live Till I Die", then she went into the Italian version of "Love Me With All Your Heart". Then, demonstrating an uncanny youthful versatility, Mia went into the handclapping, rejoiceful Havah Nagilah, with lyrics in Jewish. From this happy tune, she switched to the tear-rendering, emotion - packed "Mama", completely in Italian to the delight of the mixed audience. Finally, Mia brought the crowd back to a finger-snapping mood by closing off with a steamrolling, swashbuckling version of Bill Bailey, with the full treatment of a veteran Broadway musical performer.

This teenage Lansdowne entertainer must be seen and heard. She has poise, tonal quality and timing, and her phrasing is immaculate. You'd think she'd been around for

MIA MORRELL
... she took the stage

years. All in all, you might say it was a proud night both for South Philadelphia and Delaware County.

* * *

Notes: Sick Call: Spencer Videon, Sr. is in Delaware County Hospital, room 344... Keeping It In The Family: The recent Lion Club Drawing was won by local Lion Club President John H. Nagel's mother ... Liaison Officer for the Air Force Academy is a Colonel Gonzales, an Upper Darby High School grad, year 1937 ... Rabbi Jerome Weistrop of the Temple Israel Synagogue, will discuss the "Jewish View Of Death" tomorrow night in his series of Friday night discussions ... Mary Ann Washco of Bywood is Director of Public Relations for the American Institute For Italian Culture, which will present Dr. Max M. Leon, President of Philadelphia Grand Opera Co. and radio station WDAS, in an outline of the history of Italian operas ... When banker Al Grace was hospitalized recently, the Optimist Club president of the local U. D. group received visits from club member Dr. Hinton, who "wanted to put me in an oxygen tent", and from former club president Paul Trump, local undertaker, "who showed up with a tape measure, black suit and order book". "Great for the morale", announced prez Grace, who is now out of the hospital and back at the Girard Company Bank at 69th and Market Sts. ...Martin Conner, who retired from the Pennsylvania State Employment Service after 29 years of service, was feted at the local Shack Restaurant last Thursday, and was surprised to see an old friend, Bob Meeker, who worked with him many years ago in the Norristown office, and is now with the Pa. Manufacturers Association ... Pianist - Composer Eddie De Luca of Drexel Hill, is appearing at the Alpha Club in Philly with two other locals, Earl Hollis and Jim Malone. Eddie, who writes and records for the Somerset Label, and had authored two Albums, Conquerors Of The Ages, and Safari, has a new and exciting Concerto, due to come out in March by the Hollywood, Calif. recording company ... Vocalist Mia Morrell's dad, Arturo, is featured pianist at the Lorelei Room, an intimate cocktail lounge behind the Shubert Theater building off Broad St. in center city ...

Attendance Reported For Skating Rinks

Robert H. Taggart, recreation chairman for the Haverford Twp. board of school directors, reported at the Jan. 13 meeting an estimated attendance at Haverford's six ice skating areas and a Friday Night Teen-age dance to be well over 1,300.

A one-night inspection of the various skating areas by members of the recreation advisory board showed about 800 adults and youth enjoying an evening of outdoor fun. During the same week more than 600 teen-agers attended the Friday night teen-age dance held in the junior high gym.

Attendance figures for the basketball leagues were not included in the above estimates. Basketball is offered to men and boys of Haverford Township every Saturday morning and afternoon.

It's his 26th Annual Copa Appearance...

He must be doing something right!

JULES PODELL presents

JOE E. LEWIS
(AUSTIN MACK at the Piano)

MIA MORRELL

BILL SELBY ★ ROBERTA CARR
The World Famous Copa Girls

JOSEPH MELE and the COPACABANA ORCHESTRA
FRANK MARTI and the COPA CHA-CHA BAND

Staged by DOUG COUDY
Music & Lyrics by JOCK CASASUS
Orchestrations by JOSEPH MELE
Costumes designed by ALVIN COLT
Executed by MME. BERTHE
Coiffures by LARRY MATHEWS
Jewelry by CORO and VENDOME

Member of the Diners' Club

COPACABANA
10 E. 60th ST. AIR CONDITIONED Plaza 8-0900

I HAD GRADUATED

from High School

AND A YEAR LATER

I PLAYED THE COPA IN NEW YORK

Mia Morrell Is Big on Power

NEW YORK—Big surprises come in little packages and United Artists songstress Mia Morrell is no exception. The newly signed artist, appearing on the same bill with Joe E. Lewis at the Copacabana, may be small in stature, but she possesses a powerful voice.

Leading with "Nothing Can Stop Me Now," Miss Morrell displayed a deep and distinctive style. Her approach and style is similar to Shirley Bassey, but she injects enough of her own touch.

Miss Morrell performed only standards in this outing. Her numbers included "Put on a Happy Face," "I Enjoy Being a Girl" and "The Trolley Song." She presented "Hava Nagila" in different tempos, ranging from a pensive, deliberating opening to that of a spirited, rousing conclusion. **HANK FOX**

Billboard

Signings

United Artists Records has signed **Ike Cole,** younger brother of **Nat Cole,** and the **Gurus** to long-term contracts. . . . . The

stage of th
harder and
songs that
corded. Vocali:
terial will na.
best for themse

Harrison has r
from John Phillip
Lennon-McCartne
Dylan.

"I hope I'll new

Vaude, Cafe Dates

New York

Mia Morell tapped for the singing spot on the Joe E. Lewis show opening the season at the Copacabana Sept. 8 for three weeks . . . George Burns to play the Nugget, Sparks, Nev., starting June . . . three weeks. The D—— Pipers on the bill wi—— . . . Sergio Franch—— Sahara, Las Ve—— weeks . . . P—— Monticell—— Oct. 2—— the ——

London, sta—— Gary to—— Juan—— to

——Miami Beach, June —— Dorothy I——

SEPTEMBER 12, 1966

Between The Act——

Post Call At The Copa

By DAN LEWIS
Staff Writer)
—— York—Breathlessly,
—— time for barl call her
At Aqueduct Nah. —— the Copacaban
—— solely for Joe E. Lewis's
—— 26th annual outing thi——
—— (traditionally opens the New York
—— there he E. stands in ——
—— diminish he recorded verific——
—— that Joe E.'s name ——
—— straight openings in the——
—— ceeded for ——
The —— other night ——
—— crowded room —— waiting in ——
90— optimistic, and everyone knew Joe E.
an —— good time onto the Copa ——

——— seem to store up energy
—— for the big blast out every time
—— when he arrives at the Copa
—— He did not disappoint them ——an
—— —— funny lines as well as loose —
—— Preceding Lewis was Mia ——
—— Elizabeth —— singer, making her Copa debut
—— Leslie U—— she has a pretty voice ——
——, Sept. 7 —— far in her arrangement, under the dire——
—— scheduled f—— Norman ——
—— ton, Nov. 14 —— excel ——
down for the Copa —— young ——
—— Marguerite Pia —— She ——
at Caesar's Palace, —— however, ——
the fall. —— waiting ——
Tony Lavelli —— could hear that ——
show at the Robi —— nun drop while ——
Arden, Del. July —— ——
Randall lined up —— ——
Evergreen Park, —— ——
Nino Tempo & A—— ——
—— r the Chevron ——
—— y 25. Nick C—— ——
—— eograph N—— ——
—— at the —— ——
—— Aug. —— ——
—— Hun—— ——
—— Ju—— ——
—— eg—— ——

Fort Worth Press, Sunday, July 28, 196——

10-B

Due at Club

Mia Morell, singer with a sultry style, opens at Casa del Sol Monday, to be there through next Saturday. The Bill Swift Combo will accompany her.

PERRY STEW——

Tarnishe—— Image?

Gossip from over the backlot fence, and else—— Filmdom is beginning to wonder if Richard —— appeal as a leading man will be tarnished afte—— trays a mild-mannered, middle-aged, homosexual —— the film version of "Staircase." (They might ask —— of Rex Harrison, who'll play opposite Burton, or —— lach of the Broadway version).

Did you really think John Huston would let s—— else play his daughter's daddy in "A Walk With Lo—— Death"? Latest word f——m 20th Century-Fox is t—— —— veteran director has cast himself as the nobleman fathe—— of his daughter, Anjelica . . . Harold Emery says of —— campaign speech by the governor of New York: "It wa—— typically Rockefeller — had all the standard oil."

* * *

THEY'LL FILM "Patton," that roadshow epic about the —— war exploits of Old Blood-and-Guts, in Spain. (Because —— there's a large stock of WW II equipment there, that's —— why.) Franklin J. Schaffner ("Planet of the Apes") will —— direct George C. Scott in the role . . . Today will be —— your last opportunity to hear Peter Falk sing "Ciao, —— Ciao Blackbird." The Worth Theater is jerking "Anzio" to —— make way for "Dark of the Sun," a Rod Taylor-Yvette —— Mimieux film.

"Rosemary's Baby," a hauntingly marvelous piece of —— cinema which this column caught on the West Coast re—— cently, will come to the Ridglea Theater Aug. 7. It's Oscar —— bait for Mia Farrow and Ruth Gordon.

THE NOCTURNAL JOURNAL: Mia Morell, the petite —— songstress playing Casa del Sol this week, is probably the —— best thing that has happened to the miniskirt since rip—— away seams. She has a compact, zestful little act character—— ized by smartly arranged medleys. Standards like "Secret —— Love" and "Shadow of Your Smile" are show-cased well, —— with only a little too much brass from Bill Swift's combo.

The two most refreshing tunes in Miss Morell's show —— are an oldie-but-goodie ("The Trolley Song") and a fresh, —— switched-on new one ("I Have a Mind of My Own"). —— Swinging a close second is the soulful medley of —— "Sometimes I Feel Like a Motherless Child" and "Look —— Down That Lonesome Road." (Of course, you have to ig—— nore the incongruity of a well-scrubbed, 98-pound blonde —— singing that she's weary a-totin' that heavy load.)

GOOD NEWS DEPT.: John Autry's marathon (Seven —— nights weekly) engagement at the Town Pump piano bar —— and David Hanson's return to Mama Dorothy's Roadrunner —— Club——News —— ——"——Sec——d" is the Worth Hotel —— "Sometimes I Feel Like a Motherless Child—— —— Down That Lonesome Road—— —— nore the in——

MY STAGE NAME BECAME Mia Morrell.

It's a wig - Managers or agents wanted me to cut my hair - no way - so I wore a wig for a short time.

'1960's

THE JERRY BLAVIT TV SHOW

New Acts

MIO MORRELL
Songs
16 Mins.
Copacabana, N.Y.

Mia Morrell is an attractive youngster who has been given one of the choicer slots at the Copacabana. Being on the premiere show of the season on the bill with Joe E. Lewis is one of the best showcasings of the year.

Unfortunately, Miss Morrell needs much more experience to make an appearance count for the most on such a site. She has a deep-set voice, which is hard to control with her slight build. Her songs haven't been well selected either. With her type of delivery, they are more suited to club dates, and her couturiering isn't too flattering.

However, there are saving graces. She is personable, moves well around the floor and there are times when Miss Morrell almost seems to make it here! But more seasoning is called for. *Jose.*

PHYLLIS McGUIRE
Songs
50 Mins.
Act IV, Detroit

The one in the middle of the McGuire Sisters, Phyllis is soloing for the first time and, as might be expected, she's got it made — even without wings. Without Dot and Chris on her flanks, she displays a custom-made, cleverly-arranged songalog that has Las Vegas and other top spots clearly in mind.

It seems almost superfluous to point out that Phyllis McGuire can sing—alone, or in a trio. She belts 'em, melts 'em, twists 'em and gags 'em up; she does polished impressions—bally and via mannerisms— Judy Garland, Rosemary Clooney, Eartha Kitt, Ethel Merman, Louis Armstrong.

She is such a versatile performer that it's curious why sharp producer hasn't discovered all her talents and put her in musical comedy. She has the personality and the ability.

Handwritten note: "O-BSIE - I BAD ONE"

Handwritten note: "The Tonight Show / Yes, with Johnny Carson"

Documentaries ━ Continued from page 32

So You Want To Be A Star?

WITH THE ARRIVAL of the Beatles on the entertainment scene four years ago, a new concept of show business was born — that it wasn't necessary, anymore, to submit to the gruelling grind of the vaudeville and night club circuit for years to get to the top; all you had to have was looks, brains, youth—and talent. But one thing the teens aspiring for stardom overlooked was the fact that once the pinnacle is reached, the grind is still there; the plane-and-train hops from city to city; light snacks eaten hastily between or after shows; the three-a-day appearances, sometimes under the most adverse circumstances; disappointing audiences in out-of-the-way bistros; endless rehearsals; a dozen costume changes each night — and, always, the nagging fear, "Was I good enough tonight?" At Mangam's Chateau, Lyons, last week, an 18-year-old singer named Mia Morrell, who has been on the night club circuit on the east coast for almost two years, finally took a gigantic stride upward when she signed a three-year contract with William Morris, one of the world's largest booking agencies, and also with United Artists to make records. Has the past two years of struggle been worth it? Yes, Mia says, although in these photos she runs through the gamut of an average evening in show business—a gamut that would stagger a lesser person. The night begins, of course, with putting on her own makeup in a small dressing room backstage, after which her mother, Dancer Diane Waters, who travels with her, zips up the gown in which she will make her initial appearance on stage. Between shows (upper right) she discusses legalities with Mrs. Helen Mangam, her "boss" until June 10, while Alfred G. Roy, manager of the Chateau, and Vera Roy, hostess, look on. At the lower left, she gets together with members of the show's troupe to "tighten up" the evening's show. They are (seated, left to right) Dee Dee Prince, Ronnie Del, Mia and Comedian Ken Barry, and standing are Singer Bob D'Fano and Dancer Henry Boyer. With the midnight show set, Mia relaxes long enough to try a quick bowl of rice pudding with her mother in a secluded corner of the club's dining room, then, a hasty costume change 20 minutes later, she goes into her opening number. As a curtain ringer, she dons the "Raggedy Ann" garb popularized by another youngster who made it—Judy Garland—as she sings "Over the Rainbow." That's all for the night, and it's back to a hotel room shared with her mother, but it's a routine that continues seven nights a week, without let-up. So you want to be a star, teenager? If you do, the big question is, of course, "Can you take it?"

(LIFE Photos by Sean O'Gera)

Chicago Tribune
Sunday, May ... 1964

7th A...

DUKE ELLINGTON will bring his famed orchestra to Chicago's Opera House to appear in concert Thursday, April 28, 8:30 p.m., in their only Chicago concert of the season. Tickets from $3 to $6 are available at Allied Arts, 20 N. Wacker and all Sears stores.

It's the lucky ...sary for the Di... er's famous re... lounge at 5700 N... trio of persona... Rocco, Guy ar... adding zest to... by presenting... champagne t... guests nightly... 3, Wednesday... day, May 5 a... 6, You are h... the fun and... their lucky week.

Di Leo's... have been... success eve... first day of... customers I... to Di Leo's... both physic... tige. In tl... many Chic... and dined...

THE LERNER NEWSPAPERS

PLEASURE

...Chicago!, dining and e...

On the Town

At Mangam's Chateau

THE last of the night clubs with a line of dancing girls, a show comprising half a dozen acts and several changes of costume, dancing, and dining—the way it used to be in the good old nights—is Mangam's Chateau, on Ogden avenue in Lyons. Its new revue is no more original in content than its title, "Hollywood or Bust," but it is busting with old fashioned entertainment. There's even a lady tap dancer, the first these eyes have seen in a night club in many moons.

There are singers and dancers, burlesque clowns with pies in the face, high kickers and good lookers, balloons and buffoonery, and an exciting young girl singer who gives promise of great things to be heard. She is Mia Morrell, a tiny but sturdy soprano with a voice as true as a Greenwich time signal and the biggest, bluest eyes of the month. She hails from Lansdowne, Pa. [home town of the late Eddie Collins, a Hall of Fame second baseman of whom she says she never has heard], she has been singing around Philadelphia, she likes to belt solid numbers like "Bill Bailey" and "Ma, He's Makin' Eyes at Me," cuddles an Italian ballad, "Mama," and is by far the most exciting thing in the big, brassy show.

...the spec...
is supreme of fruit a...

THE FABULOUS Exceptions, Mercury Record Stars, are the top feature at the popular Club Laurel. This is an all Chicago unit that has gained fame throughout the country. The Laurel has musical entertainment and dancing every night. No cover or admission charge is made.

...YOUNG, talented Mia Morrell makes her Chicagoland debut as the femme singing star of the rollicking, funny new colorful revue "Hollywood or Bust" burlesque revue ...Mangam's Chateau...

Mangam's
CHATEAU

Mad Mother of Mirth
Phyllis
Diller
Sixty Hilarious M...

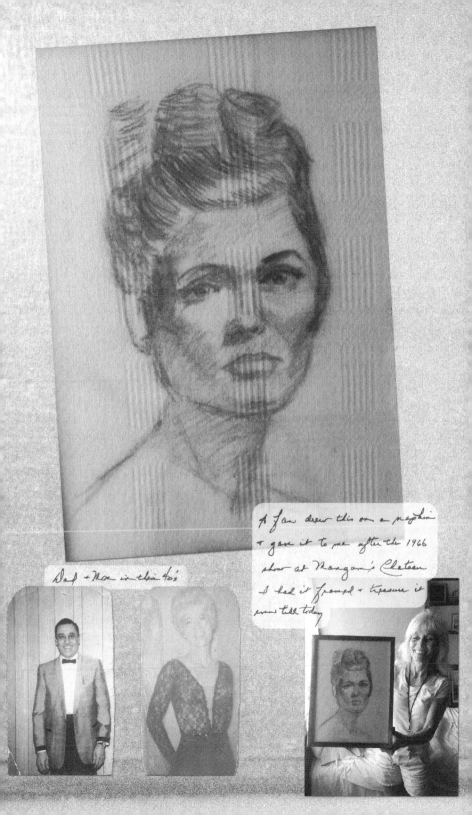

A fan drew this on a napkin
+ gave it to me after the 1966
show at Mangam's Chateau
I had it framed + treasure it
even till today

Dad + Mom in their 40's

THE BIGGEST SHOW EVER STAGED IN PHILADELPHIA

18-HOURS OF TOP ENTERTAINMENT

THE VARIETY CLUB TELETHON

ON WFIL-TV 6

Starting Saturday night at 10:30 . . . Straight through to Sunday afternoon

— IN PERSON—LIVE—DIRECT FROM TOWN HALL —

- BOBBY RYDELL
- LARRY STORCH
- FABIAN
- AL MARTINO

- DAVE GARROWAY
- MIA MORRELL
- AL ALBERTS
- JACK SMITH

- HUGH O'BRIAN
- BILLY LEE
- SALLI SACKSE
- COCO THE CLOWN

- PATTI PAGE
- DR. JOYCE BRO
- VIRGINIA GIBSO

the Broadway show "Hair" and
...

'air'

erform—
some May,
...ndles
add—
The

Bombshell at Persian

Mia Morrell, the beautiful "Sex-Bombshell of Song," is feautured in the fast-moving "Sensuously Yours" revue at the Persian Room, Marco Polo Hotel. Her arrangements and songstylings are nightly showstoppers in this bold, brash revue with a cast of 26. There are two shows nightly, 9 and 12 midnight.

* * *

Mia Morrell
at the
Persian Room.

WHEN I FIRST CAME TO L.A. I GOT A
NEW LOOK
I GOT BLONDE

SIGHTS AND SOUNDS: Three busy days ended yesterday for Steve Allen, here on a promo visit for WFIL-TV. At the Bellevue, Steve taped a 30-minute version of his syndicated TV show for airing locally at a later date. One of the featured performers was local songstress **Mia Morrell.** After listening to her vocal stylings, Steve said he would invite her to perform on his regular show. From the Bellevue, Steve went to Wanamakers to autograph books and records. His weekend itinerary also included visits to Chester County for a benefit for Rush Hospital, an interview on Frank Ford's WPEN radio show and a visit to the Methodist Home for Children.

OUT AND ABOUT: Coincidental with the opening of "Jimmy" last night at the Forrest was a visit by William R. (Will) Fowler, press agent for the "Daniel Boone" TV series. Will is the son of Gene Fowler, author of "Beau James," the novel on which "Jimmy" is based. He was unable to see the show because he and Roosevelt (Rosey) Grier, newest addition to the videseries, had to jet to Miami to continue their promo tour. Grier guested on Mia...

MIA MORRELL
. . . sings for Steve

Carter Throws His Barbs at Many Targets

By ARNOLD S. HIRSCH

So... In his hilarious rambl... Car-
his op... e of
Cali-
less
le
less

JACK CARTER
Jabs and Jibes

MIAMI HERALD

By GEORGE BOURKE
Herald Amusement Editor

• • • •

Opening the Diplomat
show is Mia Morrell, who
serves notice with the quality of her song and the electri-
city of her personality that
she'll be in the closing stellar
spot next time around.

And she will. Unless her
managers decide to bring her
along slowly on strong supporting bills for a year or so.

If such is the strategy we
hope they don't tamper too
much with the image on
view at the Diplomat. The
still-in-her-teens miss has a
smile that's worth a thousand songs.

Vocally, she has great versatility, scoring with a plain-
tive "Secret Love" and "Ask
How Much I Love You"; the
heart-throb of schmaltz in
songs about mother and with
ethnic appeal, and in the
challenge of "Nothing Can
Stop Me Now."

In the last she convinces
that Warner's may have an
Oscar winner this coming
April. Every number pleases
— but in the final analysis,
as it goes now, Mia does
more for the songs than the
total of their grouping does
for Mia.

* * *

Men...
Day...

Male m...
manded...
the Mich
theaters
them.

The tw...
ters h a v...
Men's D...
noons. M...
titled to...
a cup of
doughnut...

Since...
Day pro...
Wednesd...
ago, the...
ceived a...
of reque...
folk ask...
benefits...
Now t...

THE MIAMI NEWS
Saturday, Nov. 26, 1966 7-

Mia (New)
And Jessel
Both Score

The Diplomat has started
its winter nightclub season
with something old, some-
thing new — George Jessel
and singer Mia Morrell.

Miss Morrell, a pretty little thing with sparkling blue
eyes, lightish brown hair
that falls half way to her
waistline and a peaches and
cream complexion, is the
new face and voice and a
fresh catalog of songs. Except for "Hava Nagila" her
repertoire consists of numbers that haven't been sung
to death. Even with "The
Twelfth of Never," she intro-
duces it with the folk lyrics
that were original. Her best
is "My Mama" sung in Eng-
lish and Italian. It's a ten-
der and affectionate song
and she delivers it with feeling—**HERB KELLY**

."
ing to town," he continued.
"Well, at least they won't have
a transportation p r o b l e m.
They'll just walk on the water."

Carter himself had...

..."
in those tight pants! I don't
know why they just don't paint
their legs black and lace up
their dirty toes."

Carter also did a surprisingly
good impression of Richard
Burton reading poetry and his
own capsule version of "Fiddler
on the Roof" that should have
Zero Mostel plucking his beard.

* * * *

FEATURED with the veteran
Carter is Mia Morrell, a 19-
year-old songstress who has
astonishing poise and stage
presence to go along with her
wide-spectrum singing ability.

On the brink of the big time,
Miss Morrell has just signed
with one of the large talent
agencies and a major recording company.

Detroiters who m i s s e d the
chance to see Barbra Streisand
in her pre-stardom days at the
Caucus Club would be well ad-
vised to catch Miss Morrell.
She seems destined to go far.

Her father, incidentally, led a
Latin-American d a n c e band
here for years, many of them
at the old Famous Door. He
used the name Arturo, but his
real name is Arthur Waters.

For that matter, Mia's real
name is Marquita Waters. The
Mia is a contraction of Marquita, and Morrell is her dancer-
mother's maiden name.

Both Carter and Miss Morrell
will be at the Roostertail for
two weeks.

rock 'n roll groups

NIGHTCLUBREVIEW

PLAYBOY CLUB
Penthouse Room

Whether it is through the efforts
of the Playboy Club or the last few
singers in the Penthouse Room,
staging of late has been both inven-
tive and fresh, and talent has abound-
ed. Mia Morrell, the current attrac-
tion, does more than her share to keep
the streak going. Starting her first
number, "Nothing Can Stop Me Now,"
off-stage, with no microphone, she
belts a song like Ethel Merman, and
the sound comes in a five-foot pack-
age. She has all of the new, "in" trap-
pings as witnessed by an original,
"Mind of My Own," which she has
just recorded. Her ability to hit and
hold almost makes one envision the
high mountains she is shouting from
when she sings "Secret Love."

A spiritual medley she ran through
included "Sometimes I Feel Like A
Motherless Child" and "Look Down
That Lonesome Road," with feeling
that showed an inward perspective
into the meaning of the words. Her
m o v e m e n t s are those of a
subdued go-go dancer straining to
break loose. She is the type of woman
one calls on when a well-rounded singer is needed, capable of lusty ballads,
contemporary up-tempo, or spirituals.
She leaves one with the feeling she
has more in her bag than the 30 minutes or so allowed her to show.

AKEN TO CLINIC —
Baroness A f d e r a Fran-
chetti, former wife of actor
Henry Fonda, suffering
from a heart condition, is
accompanied by a detective
to a medical clinic in Rome.
The baroness was arrested
Aug. 1 on charges of smug-
gling 50 grams of mari-
juana from London to Italy.
—UPI Photo.

chairman...
city to join...
month will...
board to pla...
lion dollar pr...
vember ball...
referendum.

City spokesm...
yesterday they...
a final decisio...
engineering an...
from their cor...

The city is...
with the Sagina...
supply system...
partner in that...
uses Whitestone...
Tawas as its ra...

Nixon Sh

HONG KON
(UPI)—Former
dent Richard
shopping and s...
yesterday. His...

"SOFT SKIN"

STONE 2511
WOODWARD
AT HENRY

BOLD RACY

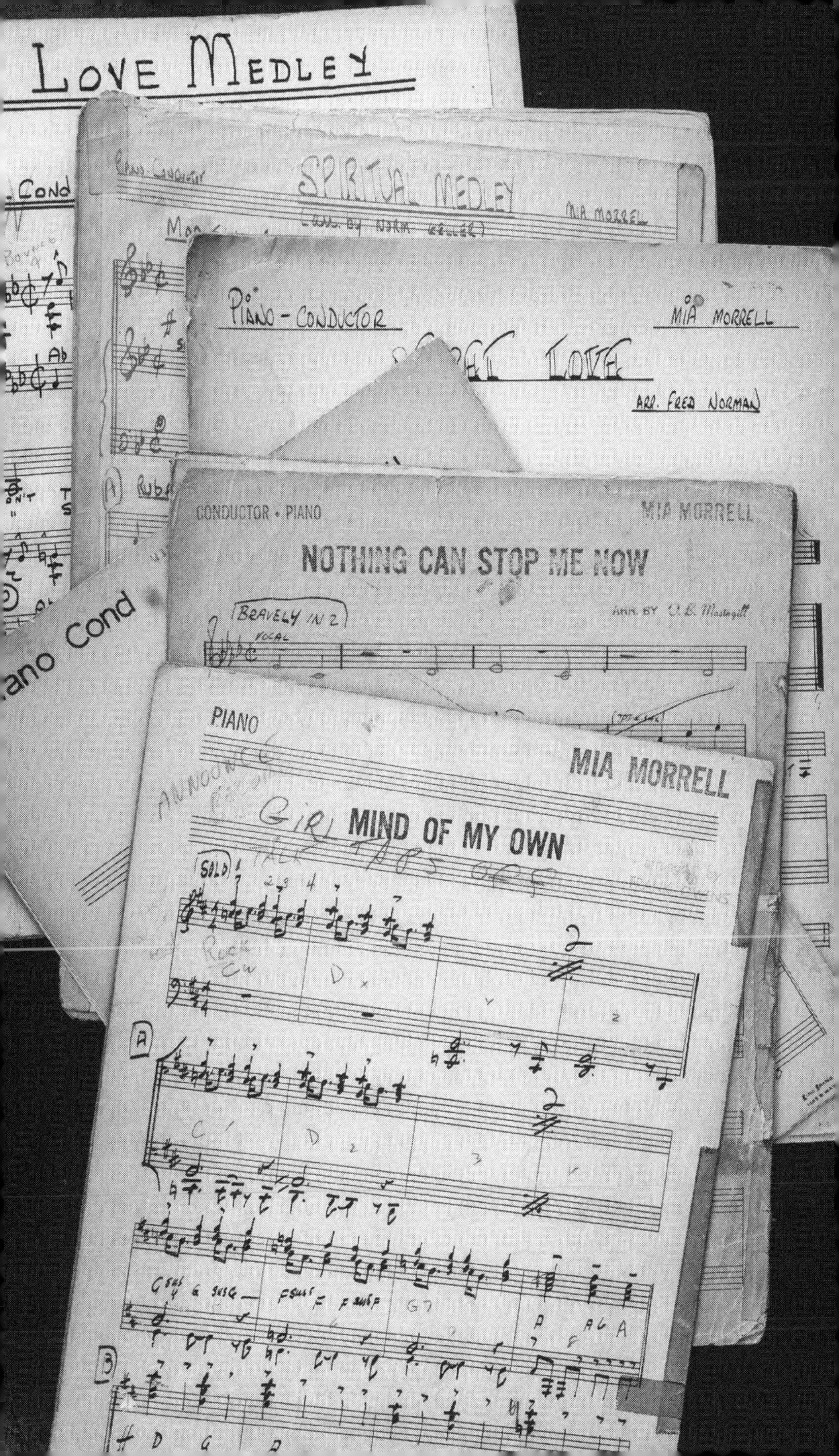
LOVE MEDLEY
SPIRITUAL MEDLEY
MIA MORRELL
PIANO - CONDUCTOR
MIA MORRELL
ARR. FRED NORMAN
CONDUCTOR • PIANO
MIA MORRELL
NOTHING CAN STOP ME NOW
BRAVELY IN 2
VOCAL
PIANO
MIA MORRELL
MIND OF MY OWN
SOLO

HURRICANE EAST   1970's

WILDWOOD, NEW JERSEY

1970's

Tom Keegan took all these pictures
at the Wine Cellar, Philly

Steppi...

...music, you're in for a very ... in Pennsauken, ... knock - down - drag ... out BA... ...esday night, feat-... ...th the best ... ...sic. This week, they ... ...ally known BLUE ... GR... ...have... come from ... Was... fav... ...k for a rousing, exciting ... al...st ... ...in this spacious and friendly establishment ... Wednesday night.

...BOB CORSEY... happy to know that Bob is now ... sounds at the LEOPARD LOUNGE ... &... ts, Pa., ...e Wednesday, Thurs... ...In ...dition the average ... ...d ... by MONTAGE sounds ... ...great appreciation.

The ... ...other le... ...SQUITA WATERS ... ...out WATT SQUEEZE has ushered ... ...thaw at the Jersey shore ... ...S TAVERN in Cape May. This ... ...rgy and the group is very hot. M...q... ...and her music continue to grow stronger ... ...better. It's worth the drive from Philly ... ...a glimpse and feast your eyes and ears on ... ...lovely lady.

The THUNDER VALLEY INN, in Cornwell... Heights, Pa., is presenting MODERN IMAGE fo... ...the next couple of weeks, and a special on Mon... day... ...night featuring the fabulous JOAN ROD... GER...UO.

...DISCO WORLD in ...nsauken, N.J., contin...he ...er their policy of ... and entertainment. Th... week, THE TRAMMP... ...be appearing on We... ...day night only. Th... ...s of room for f... and dancing at this ... ...see for yours... Watch ... DI... ...Show with ... ...ON JOSEPH ... ...morning at 10... A.M. ...annel 17 ... ...nder of the w... D... ...presses L... ...FLESH and ... T...sda... ...ight ... ...ce instructions for ... ...one in...d.

BLU... is co... item... cob...

N.J., accep... lishi... terta... Crab... HAR...

...r ...LEE... NAI...

...MESQUITA WATERS

MARQUITA

MARQUITA

MARQUITA

VOICE OVER / VOCAL TAPE   TIME: 2:57   AFTRA
1. Intro-Giggler   5. Young Boy   9. Excit-Slinghsy/Goofy
2. Busy   6. Grandmother   10. VOCAL
3. Excited   7. Teen
4. Intimate/Sexy   8. Sincere/Mom

I Got a First Photo Shoot for
The Best Laugh in My
Voice Over Class

CAUGHT IN THE ACT

Shaw at Vine St. Bar and Grill

No doubt enticed by Vine St. Bar and Grill's reputation for catering to soulful, sultry sirens, Marlena Shaw and Jessica Smith — two songstresses of variable talent — appeared at the cushy supper club on separate occasions.

Saucy, yet infectious, imposing, yet sexy, Shaw is your ideal jazz-r&b composite. Her husky alto induces comparisons to Nancy Wilson and Sarah Vaughen, but still is scented with its own distinct nuance.

Backed by a trio — which included renowned session bassist Phil Upchurch — Shaw flashed impeccable taste in material and an intuitive grasp of phrasing. When blessed with a supple set of pipes it is tempting for a performer to spend an entire set wasting notes and swimming through a sea of histrionics. There was a little showing off, yet Shaw's real forte is reconstructing mediocre material and turning it into heart-stopping lyrical statements.

Take the Patty Austin-James Ingram pop hit "Come to Me," for example. On record, this love letter drags to a medium tempo. However, in Shaw's hands, the song sparks with a raging lust that the recorded version does not come close to mustering.

During the 45-minute set, Shaw and company also heaved through some blues and whipped up a few snappy jazz standards. Shaw will return to Vine St. (1610 N. Vine St., Hollywood) in march.

* * *

Ethereal, not snappy, is the word that best describes Jessica Smith. Armed with a scrape-the-sky soprano on the order of Deniece Williams, this affable vocalist conjures up some pleasant,

MARLENA SHAW
Jazz-r&b songstress

soothing imagery on tunes like the Motels' "Only the Lonely."

Nevertheless, the song lacks the urgency and dispair of the original. Other tunes also lacked spark, undermined by unimaginative arrangements.

* * *

Imagination and sparks were flying at Josephina's (13602 Ventura Blvd. Sherman Oaks), however on a recent Monday evening, the night the Rick Hones Band delivers its smoldering top-forty r&b hits from its side dish of fusion.

Although the band played well, it was guest singer Marquita Waters who fills in occasionally, that was responsible for the vocal fireworks.

Equally enamored of r&b, pop and jazz, Waters' piercing, yet sonorous voice flushes out every ounce of emotion a ballad like "Just Once" contains. Veering into jazz, she chiseled out a version of "Night in Tunisia" that would have Dizzy Gillespie reeling.

— Kevin Henry

MOM WAS STILL DANCING IN HER
LATE 60's + 70's

Running taught
me many things.
I learned that
I could finish
what I said
I would do.

I learned
I was a winner

MAR 26, 1994

Someone Special

Marquita

Bobby

I MINISTERED TO BOYS AT A
MIDIUM SECURITY CAMP
FOR ABOUT 8 YEARS
I SANG AND PREACHED

BUDDY WAS ON THE FREEWAY + TIGER WAS LIVING IN THE WAS WHEN I RESCUED THEM.

I RESCUED BUDDY WHEN HE WAS DUMPED AT THE SOCCER FIELD NEAR MY HOME

1990's Singing at Students Show

This STUDENT WAS RECORDING
AN ALBUM JUST FOR HER FAMILY

KID'S I KNOW WE DROVE THE BAND
NUTS - SO MUCH FUN

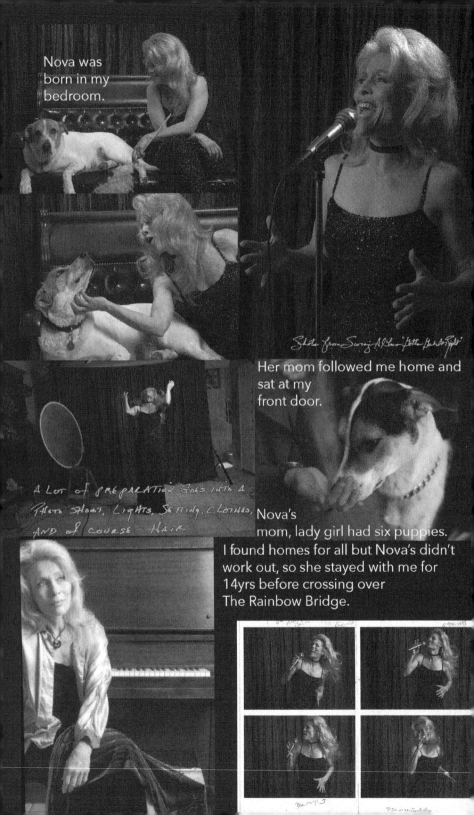

Nova was born in my bedroom.

Her mom followed me home and sat at my front door.

A LOT of PREPARATION GOES INTO A PHOTO SHOOT, LIGHTS, SETTING, CLOTHES, AND of COURSE - HAIR

Nova's mom, lady girl had six puppies. I found homes for all but Nova's didn't work out, so she stayed with me for 14yrs before crossing over The Rainbow Bridge.

"When you do a cover song,
Make it your own."

"Stay"
-Rihanna

"On My Knees"
-Jaci Velasquez

"Try"
-P!nk

WHEN WE SHOT THE VIDEO for
"I WILL NOT GROW WEARY" WE
PICKED ONE SPOT I WALK TO EACH DAY

FROM THE MUSIC VIDEO
PRODUCED + DIRECTED BY ANN GILAN

original "CHRIST"

from the Music Video for "Christ
Produced ~ Directed by Ava Gehn

Tips for the Voice

PERFORMANCE PRACTICE

IS A GREAT WAY

TO GET READY FOR SHOWS

THE STUDIO IS MY SECOND HOME
The stage is my first

NU GUNN playing
ss on "Christ" at
ark Vincent's Studio

MARK J. VINCENT
Engineer, Producer:
"Gotta Get It Right"
"Walking With God"
Engineer: "Christ"

MARQUITA with ANU who did the book cover
design, photography & scrapbook design.

MARQUITA & SCOTT FRANKFURT
during the mixing and mastering of "Christ"

*As we walk through our lives let us not stay
in the Valley of Wishing and Hoping but go
to the Summit of Doing and Done.*

PART II

How To Sing Through It All

E veryone should be careful with their voice. But when this is what you use for your profession, then it becomes necessary to care for your voice even more. When you speak you are using the same muscles as the ones for singing. So your speaking voice has to be considered in reference to how it affects your sound. You can be speaking too low or high, and not breathing enough. Maybe you're getting hoarse or tired after speaking. Whenever someone comes to me for singing lessons, I always take note of their speaking to see if there are problems. If there are, they will tire your voice and leave you with bad habits. In severe cases there can be damage to the vocal folds. Unlike a guitar, you can't change those strings, so to speak. Your instrument is living in you; you take it everywhere. Just imagine an instrument that you carried around with you, and how it would look after a while. You carry your voice everywhere and use it in every kind of situation. Even when you aren't singing or speaking, it is influenced when you are emotional (good or bad), doing business, arguing, shouting, or laughing. Start to monitor how your speaking voice sounds.

Optimum Pitch

We speak around a certain pitch, and there is the possibility that yours is too low or too high. Your optimum pitch is the one you speak at that gives you the most sound for the least amount of energy. It is the best for your voice because it is the least stressful. Part of my assessment with new clients includes evaluating their pitch center.

When things happen like stress, sickness, upsetment, partying, shouting, etc., your voice is along on that ride and expresses you. It takes the brunt of what you are going through and experiencing. When you are tired, you can start to vocally slouch. Your voice slides down to a pitch that only fries it. It becomes gravely sounding because it is too low. Your voice is carrying your tiredness in its sound. You get mad and raise your voice and possibly strain. When you're out and excited at a party, game, or park - you shout, and again you can push the muscles too far. Whatever the case, it is crucial that we take note of where (what pitch) we are speaking, so that we don't use up our voices uselessly. Instead let's save our vocal energies and muscles for singing. Wahoo, so much better.

After a long bout with a cold or flu, especially with a lot of coughing, you can start a bad habit of keeping a tired vocal sound, a lowered sound to the point of it being gravely. Speak slowly and take more breaths, but also raise the pitch to where it is clear.

Many years ago I used to speak very low and never realized I was taking away from my abilities to keep my voice healthy. I kept the habit up for quite some time. After I went to voice therapy, it was so important that I kept listening to hear if I went back to dropping my voice, which I did for quite some time. I was so stubborn that it took me a year to speak at the correct pitch the therapist gave me. Then and now after many years my voice is clear and stays that way. It helps that I am constantly reminding my students about their voices. I am always monitoring to make sure they don't slide backwards, especially when they have worked to bring their voices to where they are - healthy. A bell goes off in my mind as well, reminding me to check myself and not fall back to this bad habit. I may be teaching my students, but I am always learning from them.

More Breath – Slower

When you speak, you need to remember to take in more air. Most people with vocal problems forget to breathe or don't take enough air when breathing. Holding the stomach in can be a habit that keeps you from taking a proper breath also. Most people aren't even aware they are doing it because it's a long-term habit. If this is so, then you really can't take in the air needed for speaking let alone singing. With taking too little a breath, your voice may be gravelly (rough sounding) especially at the ends of sentences. Belly breathing will help you to learn how to relax the muscles in the abdominal area and take in more air.

Belly Breathing

- Lie on the floor and put a large book on your midsection with the middle of the book at your bellybutton.
- See the book rise as you breathe in. Go slowly.
- As you leave the air out, let the book lower and again go slowly.

Belly Breathing is especially helpful in showing that you can breathe without raising the shoulders and chest. It is very soothing and will relax the muscles in the abdominal area, as well as other parts of the body.

Here is a way of practicing speaking with more air that will help. It may seem odd to do and not worth the time, but bear with me and try it. You will be so much more aware of your speech patterns than you are now... Healthy voice.

- As you raise your arm in front of you, you inhale.
- As you lower your arm you speak and with every word you move your arm down little by little.
- You are not concentrating on what you are saying. You should be more focus on taking enough air in, slowing down, and speaking at your optimum pitch.

This is hard to do because we are wrapped up in what we are saying and the emotion that it carries with it. In voice therapy, you must separate your emotion from the execution of your words. You are to be more interested in saving and bringing your voice into health than getting your emotions and point across. It can be frustrating in the beginning. Most people stop their arm and run through what they want to say. Little by little as you keep trying and realize how this is helping, you will be successful in slowing down and taking in the amount of air necessary to support what you say.

I know it's hard but work it; it works!

- Oh and not too many syllables, only 3 or 4 at first. You can do more but only after you have been successful with 3 or 4. Patience is a virtue you will be using here... Hmmm.

Nasality

If you are nasal, your uvula is down, and the tongue is up in the back of the throat. It can be either or both of these causing your nasality, but the result is that the throat is cut off and the sound goes through the nasal cavity. I describe the uvula as the punching bag in the back of the throat... everybody says "Oh yea." Recently, I have seen a lot of people that have several habits that seem to follow suit with a very nasal sound when speaking and singing. The jaw and lower lip start to be more prevalent in making sound. The lower lip is drawn into the mouth to form sounds while the top lip is kept silent and hardly involved in the process of making sound. The mouth is kept shut more than opened, and the uvula in the rear of the mouth barely moves upward. Also, the teeth are held close together when forming sound. The jaw moves forward when trying to make higher notes or louder sounds. The jaw is tensed and not relaxed.

Nasality in and of itself doesn't have to be discarded. It can be used as your style, or to pull from your bag of tricks when choosing how you want to express with your voice. We don't want to be limited by default, or do we? If you don't know how to "not be nasal" then you may want to learn how to be "open throat" then you will have the choice of how you sound. Aha, variety, the spice of life.

Getting Rid of Nasality

Use a Mirror

As you work with your voice, you will need to use a mirror a lot! It is essential that you aren't stubborn. You may think you're getting what you're working on but you need to be sure. It also helps you achieve what you are going for a lot sooner. If you don't like seeing yourself in the mirror, then it's time you did. I may seem harsh... I do mean to shake you. You want as little opposition as possible to move forward so don't sabotage yourself. First, accept where you are right now. Wear something with a great color for you that looks good. I put makeup on every day. You never know when someone will want to take a picture of you.

Yawn and Raised Uvula

A yawn is a vocal stretch. While looking in a mirror, you will be able to see if you can achieve movement of the uvula which happens naturally with a yawn.

A yawn is a vocal stretch.

Practice

- Open your mouth but don't drop the jaw too far.
- See the top teeth, as well as the side top teeth.
- Lower the jaw enough to see the back of the throat.
- Try to yawn and concentrate on the uvula in the back as well as the arches on the sides of the uvula. (Remember, it looks like a punching bag in the back of the throat, Oh yea!)
- As you yawn the uvula will rise. Feel the stretch.
- Now do a yawn again and hold the stretch.
- After being able to have some control of maintaining the stretch with the uvula lifted, and the tongue flattened (leaving an opening between the uvula and the tongue), you can proceed to the next step.
- While holding the stretch of the uvula, breath in and then out softly.
- Don't let the uvula fall. You want to start to be aware of, as well as, make your muscles used to lifting the uvula.
- Next, do precisely the same thing but instead of letting air out, make a sound.
- Keep the uvula lifted as best you can.

Remember to feel the stretch of the uvula when yawning so you know what you are going for.

Tongue Down

When you sing vowels the sound carries but when you sing consonants it doesn't. As you hold a vowel keep looking at your tongue to see if it is up too high in the back. If it is, then bring it forward slightly. Make sure the tip is facing out not under the bottom front teeth. Rounding the tongue in the front this way only makes it obstruct the opening of your mouth.

The "e" vowel is made with the tongue up in the back. You can soften its nasality by bringing the tongue forward and pressing down on the front of the tongue. Form the tongue like a slide and leave room in the back between the roof of your mouth and the tongue, just as if there would be a person at the top of a slide. Can you picture it? Good. Imagination is such a great tool!

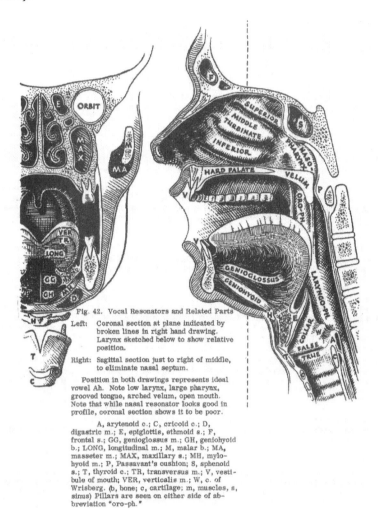

Image from "Singing, the Mechanism and the Technic" by William Vennard and used by permission from Carl Fisher Inc.

Warming Up

It happens all the time. You're singing a song and you didn't warm up. You don't need to because you're just learning a song and not pushing. The problem is that you are learning. You're practicing not warming up. Every time you go ahead like that you reinforce a bad habit. Just do a few exercises to get your muscles and blood flowing. Then you can sing some easy songs. When working on your voice, and before you go to practice a song, it makes a difference when you warm up your muscles, as well as before performances. Start with exercises that don't go to the extent of your range. You want to see how the voice feels today. Some days you may think nothing is going to come out right, but with the right coaxing it may turn out to be a great voice day. Warm up means just that, so little by little start to move higher with your exercises, and when you feel the muscles are ready, okay, then start to stretch out and work them harder.

Being Talented Can Be a Problem

When you know you can sing, the most common question is "Why do I have to vocalize? I can sing, and this is so boring. I want to get to my songs." This attitude will be a problem until you realized how significant warming up your muscles is. Don't overlook practicing just because you have a good voice, do it so you can keep that good voice and make it even better.

No Ice Please

I was backstage (in the kitchen) waiting to go on, and Tommy De Noble was there too. We were singers performing at the Drexelbrook Country Club in Philadelphia. It was a time when many places had a house band that played there regularly. They also played for the shows after dinner was served. Agents would book you and it was a thriving business. Tommy was there chomping on some ice as he talked to me. He left to go through the doors and straight to the stage to sing. I was warming up as I was next. All of a sudden there wasn't any music or singing. Tommy came running in saying, or rather struggling to say, "You have to go on, I can't sing." I just looked at him. I was startled but then ran out on stage as I realized his voice had shut down. I never forgot it. When you use ice it constricts the muscles. Tommy was doing the opposite of warming up before he went on, a big no-no. Sadly he found this out the hard way. He actually studied with my father. Tommy wanting to sound like Eddie Fisher, a star at that time, but wouldn't listen to what wisdom my father tried to impart to him. He wanted to have Tommy be an individual and have his own sound.

Remember, before singing: No carbonation, No cold drinks, and No ice. Room temperature and warm is just right. Oh and be unique, be yourself.

Note: I was thinking of performing, warming my muscles up, and centered on singing. Tommy was busy talking about anything but the subject at hand, his performance. Always be focused on your performance before entering the stage which includes the recording stage.

Youth Invades the Williamsburg Room with the appearance of Tommy DeNoble from April 6 to 11 and Marquita Waters from April 13 to 18.

Non-Singing Exercises

Not only singers but anyone who is going to use their voice more than conversationally needs these exercises. I have people say "Oh you sing, well, sing for me." I never refuse an offer to sing now, and I try to pick something that I won't hurt myself with since I'm not warmed up. I also do these exercises.

The times when you don't get to warm up but have to sing or talk (professionally speaking), you have a few minutes to do these non-singing exercises which start more blood flow. You can do them before and during vocalizing, as well as when practicing your songs if you feel a little tight.

The purpose of these exercises is not only to get the blood flowing but also to stretch the muscles in preparation for singing. You are dealing with muscles, nerve endings, blood vessels, cartilages, and ligaments. You're saying to your voice, "get ready we're gonna start working!"

Stretch/Yawn: You want to stretch as if yawning and then yawn. The only thing you might want to watch is that you don't open your mouth too long and possibly dislocate the jaw. Let the stretch of the yawn happen in the back of the throat on top. Feel how wide the back of the throat feels? See the uvula and how yawning pulls it up. It is important to note this as you will use this info not only when you're vocalizing but also when going for notes that are difficult. Yawning happens naturally when you are vocalizing correctly.

Closed Mouth Yawn: With a closed mouth, start to yawn. Keep the mouth closed as the yawn begins to form and then open your mouth. The uvula and its arches are more likely to lift without the dropping of the jaw.

Tongue Rotation: With the mouth closed, rotate the tongue in front of the teeth. Press outward, and make as big a rotation as possible. Do in both directions.

Tongue Press: With the mouth closed, press the tongue against the roof of the mouth in front of the top front teeth. Press outward, hold, and then return the tongue to its resting position. Sometimes a yawn will start which is good. When that happens, end the exercise with that yawn. Remember, open your mouth just enough as to allow the yawn to stretch the back of the throat, and take note of the wideness back there.

Tongue Rocker: You can get away with the above exercises in front of people; they'll just think you're funny looking. This one is a different story, they'll think you're crazy. Do it privately or at your own risk in front of people.

- Have the mouth open in a relaxed position, (not too long with the jaw mind you). The jaw does not move during the exercise.
- Bring the tongue out of the mouth, allowing it to drop down toward the chin. Pull it out as far as possible, but do not drop the jaw down to make the opening of the mouth longer.
- Then bring the tongue back into the mouth, with the tip curling upward along the roof of the mouth, as far back as possible.
- Now bring the tongue back out along the roof again and down to the chin.

The Tongue Rocker is a little messy, but it stretches some of the vocal fold muscles and the tongue. Notice how the thyroid cartilage moves up and down with this exercise. Again, don't move the jaw with the tongue. It stays in its open position and only the tongue moves.

Uvula Mover: Can you breathe through your nose? Some people have a tough time trying, and this exercise will have to be skipped by them for now.

With your mouth open moderately, start trying to only breathe through your nose and out through your mouth. The tongue has to stay flat and away from the uvula so that only the uvula moves when breathing in. When you do this the Uvula (the thing that looks like a punching bag in the back of your throat) will start to move up and down. It's crucial that it has this mobility to its musculature to sing high notes and to change from nasal to open throat for variety in your singing. When the uvula is down, it opens the nasal cavity to the rest of the throat. When it is up, it is closing it off. The uvula mover will take most people a considerable time to get, so be patient. Also, keep the tongue silent (not moving) and down away from the uvula. If you have a problem with nasality, this is your exercise.

Practice

Practicing Exercises

If you think that practicing exercises is boring, you are right. The only problem is that it works. If you warm up before going into the studio, you will see the difference in your performance. So how do you make sure you practice? You can try several things first, and then you may be able to tell me some ideas you come up with.

- Set a specific time and day for practice.
- Make it an appointment that you must keep.
- Practice shorter amounts of time and build the time up. It is better to practice more days than cramming in a long time one day. You are revisiting the muscles each time, building strength and memory in them. Especially if you think you can't practice because of time constraints, you will feel a lot better if you do a little, a lot more times (days). It will feel and be more doable and beneficial. No excuses - do it.
- Practice in your car - I found it so helpful to warm up my voice before going to a gig while driving, and yes it made a big difference when singing the songs. If you are in the car then utilize that time. These are the perfect moments to vocalize, warm up before a show, or go over a song and memorize lyrics. You can listen to and choose the next adventure for your repertoire. (Choose your next song.) You can do so much work there.

Mind you this doesn't take the place of looking in a mirror and being able to monitor yourself for posture, breathing, and seeing how you are opening your mouth. Let's just say that if this is the only option, then you can utilize it to the fullest and do some of your work. And when you're sitting, you are less likely to raise your shoulders or chest as you breathe in.

Some of us who have been singing for years think we don't need to check ourselves because we already have it down. I found out the hard way that I had some bad habits because of thinking and acting this way. We have to continually check to see if we are maintaining the good habits, and not developing some bad ones. Beginner or pro we need to go back to the basics and make sure they are still being done correctly. *Just do it my friends.*

"SS" - Don't Be Stubborn Stupid

You may be a great singer; you still have to practice. There are always things to learn as you continue life, and so with singing. Never get stubborn stupid, as I've called myself when I didn't practice, just because you can sing. You may have some bad habits, and you can still sing with them. Just think of how much better it would be if you fixed them. Don't be stubborn. It's stupid.

During vocalizing, you can check the mouth opening to see if the teeth are apart by putting the thumb and first finger together, and between your teeth on the side of the mouth. Also be aware that as you descend in an exercise, the tendency is to close the teeth and the mouth. Pay attention to check where your mouth opening lands, and if you are closing - then get your fingers in there.

Are you used to the exercises? You're proficient, and just need to keep the muscles exercised as all of us do? Then you can be doing some task with your hands. Sing the exercises while moving around. We need to work our muscles.

People that are studying in college or any other academic situation have very little time. Take a break and do a short amount of practice between studies. It will stimulate the brain and be a pleasant pause. When teaching kids and adults in school, they are always saying they can't practice because they have to study. I ask them why they study. They usually give me a puzzled look and say they have to. To which I reply, well this is the same. You need to do the work (study), you have to. You will be pleasantly rewarded if you practice.

No Time? Don't Believe It

Think a certain amount of time, not that you have to practice. When you feel time is limited, you will avoid practicing. Thinking of the word practice means more time than you think you have. Give yourself a limit of 5 minutes or 10 minutes. You can do that. Remember the more you visit your muscles the better it is. Do not cram a long practice in every once in a while. You may be able to get in another 5 or 10 minutes later in the day. A song is usually around 4 minutes. It all adds up and you will feel so much better. "I did it!" is so satisfying.

Muscles Have Memory

As you practice, your muscles remember the movements and adjustments you make. It is essential to give a clear picture for them as to what you want. Doing the same sound correctly a few times is better than doing it too many times, and possibly falling back to an old habit. Think it through as to how you will approach your sound and then do it. This preparation and execution done correctly will help your muscles get the picture a lot quicker. It assists them in redoing it that way again, until it is set in their memory. Always go back to basics to make sure you aren't slipping into an old bad habit, but are on top of your game.

Posture

Your posture is your approach to
life as well as your singing.

My students know the importance of keeping good posture and how it completely changes how you look. If you slouch you don't seem confident and quite possibly you aren't. When sitting and playing an instrument, it is so easy to round the back, thus making your breaths shorter and harder to support your singing. If there is no real demand in what you're singing, you can get away with it. But then again you will probably have back problems down the road. So keep a slight arch in the back and this way your ribs will more likely be lifted off the abs. You can take a good breath as well as support your voice. The added benefit - you look so much better.

You wouldn't think that just aligning the neck would make a big difference. One of my students was amazed at the difference in achieving the notes heretofore he couldn't. Goosing the neck throws off the alignment of the body and the follow through for your sound. Several of my students put their hand on the jaw to keep the neck and jaw from moving forward. By doing so, they got the higher notes they couldn't otherwise. If you have any question as to whether your jaw and neck are moving forward, just put your hand on the jaw and start to sing, that will clear things up.

Duck Stance

Check in the mirror to see how you have your legs. A lot of us tend to lock the knees and have a "duck stance." When the feet face front, one in front of the other (not parallel), and your knees are slightly bent, you are in an active mode. (Think of a boxer.) When you have your toes facing to the left and right respectively, you aren't. I call it the duck stance. It is a vulnerable stance. To move you would have to lift your foot to face and go forwards. You are going forward in life so place your toes to go straight ahead.

If you like the "power stance" where the legs are apart and parallel, and who doesn't, then bend your knees a little and make your thigh muscles work. Locking the knees creates tension. The body will compensate on your posture by moving the pelvic area forward to steady you - not good. The chest will pull down and usually the shoulders slouch. This really looks like you have no confidence. My mother was a dancer and used to drive me crazy with keeping good posture habits every day. Now I am always telling my students how important posture is and making sure they stand correctly. Thanks mom.

- Look down at your feet… are your toes facing the side?
- Have someone push on one of your shoulders in the front. You would fall back on one foot to steady yourself. It is where the body naturally goes to save you from falling, so be in that position to begin with.

"V" Legs

Another position of the legs that needs changing is when you have your feet out too far from the body, and your legs form an upside down "v." Starting from the knees going up to the top of the legs, you go inward.

- Find your pelvic bone in the front of your body towards the side, and just above each leg. Your knees and toes should be in alignment with this bone and not out any further.
- Toes forward.
- Just above the knees push the legs out from each other. No "knock knees" (knees looking at each other).
- Don't roll your feet outward when doing this.

You will see the body looking so much better, and you will have taken a lot of pressure off your knees. Try it and see how much better you look... Big smile here.

Butt Out

Standing up straight has different meanings to each of us. As we go to do it the misconceptions take form – literally. Usually I see the top of the body lifted up and the stomach pulled in. A lot of times the back is arched so much that the butt goes too far out and away from the body.

- Stand against a wall, one foot against the wall and the other slightly in front of the other like that fighter I mentioned earlier.
- Pull your butt down and try to bring your back straight against the wall.
- Keep your shoulders against the wall also. I know it feels weird but it will help.
- Correct posture is this: you should be able to stand and have an imaginary pole go straight down from the center of your head and out from between your legs. Your body should not touch the pole.

Goose Neck

The high notes are always the ones we want to get. They may be just out of reach and we unconsciously go to get them by goosing the neck (pulling the neck forward). This puts the throat out of alignment with the body and the follow through of how your sound leaves your body. Watch to see if you do this.

There are some who aren't confident they can make the note or phrase. They reach out as if to another source to get it. It isn't the case all the time. Sometimes it is just a habit you fall into. No matter what the cause, you want to work on eliminating this habit.

- Look in the mirror when singing.
- Put your hand on your chin and feel whether the neck (or jaw) is fighting you. It is your body so make your body do what you want, not what you're used to doing. It will take some time but continue to bring your neck back into alignment. Soon this will become the norm.
- Stand up straight and know with confidence you have it and can do it from within yourself.

Auditions

When you are going on an audition, the material you choose should be something you have done a million times. Maybe not a million times but you get the idea. Know the material inside out. If you just found a song you love, that is not what you do next week on an audition. After a while, I know you will hate going over and over the same dreary song. But that is what will make you pop when you audition. Seems counter to what you would think? You would think something new and exciting would do the trick, but new and exciting isn't ingrained in you. When it is ingrained and second nature you can go beyond and soar. Also, if you have to think about the words at all, you are distracted.

- The moment you step into the room - no - outside as you wait, you need to be confident, pumped.
- When you enter the room your attitude and vibe should be able to outcast any that is in the room.
- Be ready to say your name with confidence and courage.
- Go slow! So many people rush through their name. Say it slower than you want and if you are asked a question, say that a little slower than usual. Think! You may be able to express yourself with style.
- Don't drop the end of your name. The ends of sentences tend to go down usually, so be aware of this when slating (giving your name) or any dialogue.

Record yourself (video) saying your name and answering some questions like, "Where are you from?" "What are your hobbies?" Listen and see how you look, how you project and how interesting your voice is. Did you drop the ends of the sentences? Did you rush through anything you said? Keep recording until you hear the changes needed.

How are you standing? Are you standing on one leg which is straight and your hip to the side? Are your shoulders slumped forward? Are your hands in your pockets? All of these show you aren't ready! You are expressing weakness, insecurity, lack of confidence.

- Shoulders should be back showing the body in a confident and ready mode.
- Stand on both legs. It lengthens your body. Remember the fighter stance of action and readiness.
- Hands in the pockets are usually there because we don't know what to do with them. It feels comfortable but take them out. Even if you catch yourself at the audition with your hands in your pockets, slowly take them out. Practice keeping them out *when you practice.*
- Stand when you practice. Don't be fooled that you have practiced enough at home. When you are under the gun, nerves take over. Old habits and forgetting things start to happen. So practice way more than you want.
- You need "performance practice." Do it as you would at an audition: standing, looking around to imaginary people, walking, moving and making it as real as possible. Videotaping helps so don't overlook this aid. Don't just believe you have it, know for sure you do!
- If you have auditioned before and made some of these mistakes, learn from them and don't do them again. Get back in the ring and audition more.

Smile - Smile, smile, smile - show those pearly whites. It brightens up the room. Be yourself but be the best of who you are. Remember smiling and moving are great allies.

Move - Don't just stand there. Move! If it doesn't feel comfortable, then practice 'til it does. You must move when you audition because 90% or more don't. You must!

What Song - What have you been singing that you know inside-out and shows the best qualities you have? You may be so tired of this song and want to try a new one. Again, don't! As I said before, do what is tried and true. You can work on other songs, as a matter of fact, you should have around five songs that are great for you. When another song is ready, then you can use that one, but not until you know it inside-out.

What to Wear - Wear what is comfortable. Each situation may call for something a little different. Remember you want to feel that everything fits, including your clothing, so have several outfits ready that will work on the auditions you are aiming for. Always be prepared.

On Stage - This goes for when you audition and do a show. Don't wear something you will worry about while performing. If a strap keeps falling, pin it down; if a hat keeps you preoccupied, then don't wear it unless you can work it into the act. You will constantly be thinking of the item that pulls your attention. It can throw you off your concentration on auditioning and performing. Why? Don't fool yourself, it will matter and you will be sorry. Everything has to work for you, or it works against you.

Hair - If your hair is in your eyes, you can't be seen. Bangs are great but not in your eyes; unless you are the Beatles and use it as a gimmick. If you have the habit of fixing your hair as you practice, you will do it at the audition and on stage. Get used to stopping yourself from this habit. So many people say, "Oh I won't do that when I perform." The problem is you just did it while practicing your performance and you did it without even being aware that you did... Hmmm.

Look at Judges - No matter if there is one judge or several, you need to connect with them - smile. Make sure you move and look at each and every one of them. My mother used to say hit every corner of the stage. That is the best advice. Don't just stand there. Move your arms naturally but move them. If you are too nervous, look at their hair - not their eyes. The judges can't tell the difference. Do not go by what the faces of the judges look like. They may have had a bad day or are thinking of something to do later. They may even be ignoring you.

They don't decide your attitude, you do.

Be on Time - That means be early, always! Do not show up at the last minute. Planning your time so that you arrive early and get comfortable in your surroundings will be crucial. Focus your mind on what you will do. Being late is a sign you aren't really serious.

Be Yourself – Be Brave

Opportunities come your way and you must decide how you will handle them. Managers or agents may want you to be something you aren't. Go by your gut. You may be surprised at what happens. I once had an opportunity and was worried about my manager (my father) being mad. I didn't do what may have been an opportunity - you never know.

The Story...

The Merv Griffin Show was a big deal. Many celebrities came on his show, so for me having been on it many times meant a lot in the eyes of the industry. There was one time, while I was still living at home, that I was backstage waiting to go on. Mr. Griffin came up to wait also. It was cold so someone let me borrow a coat that was way too big. He dared me to go on stage with the coat. This was an opportunity to do something out of the ordinary. But, I was scared of what my father would say. I may have done the wrong thing, so I didn't go on with the coat, even though I wanted to. My father was very strict to the point of causing a lot of fear and dread. He may have been thrilled if it went well but if it didn't, I was afraid of an angry outburst when we got home. I still kept appearing on the show but never got to sit down and be interviewed. If I had taken the chance to be funny, Mr. Griffin might have called me over to sit and talk. You never know, so be brave and follow your instincts, you may be pleasantly surprised.

Psychological - Emotional

*The pain we have gone through keeps
us strong for the next incoming.*

You are captive of your bad habits and fears as well as freed by good habits and a positive outlook. Did anyone tell you, you couldn't sing? Did your siblings ask you to stop singing? When you stood out with a great big voice, did the other singers give you a look that said you better tone it down if you want to have any friends? Or did a teacher tell you to stop standing out from the rest, so that you held back your voice, and never again tried to be loud? Did you convince yourself that you just weren't as good as the next singer? My students and I have worked out these problems and more, but they had to be determined to do so.

One of my students was told by her sisters to stop singing, and she interpreted that to mean she wasn't and wouldn't be good. She kept losing the timing of the songs and didn't know where to come in on phrases. Well, it took years but she practices differently now. She realizes that she needed to listen ten times more than others, and she had to listen to the version we made, not the original singer. But in the end, she was successful and was free to have such great feeling in her songs. She worked through and passed the barriers. It may take you longer than you like, but it is worth the journey.

The other side of the coin is being too cocky about your talent and thinking you are God's gift. You can start to take for granted the talent you have and slowly lose it. Remember it's a gift. You need to respect it and work at taking care of it. The artist that takes their gift seriously, practices, and keeps focused on a good attitude is the real winner.

Vocal Problems and Performing

*Today I pray for you to know the fear that
will teach you, the courage that will move
you, and the success that will bless you.*

After I had a growth removed because of doctors injuring my
vocal folds, I was scared to hit high notes
and worried that my voice would be
damaged. I was told I was fine, but I
wasn't. I backed off instead of going for
it. Where I used to be fearless, I was gun
shy. My students were so surprised when
I'd sing for them and cracked. They never
heard me crack before. I had to get over
the embarrassment and accept where I
was vocally.

> *Worry won't solve
> the problem. It wears
> you down and keeps
> you from working a
> solution.*

You can only be the best you and the best you are at whatever
stage of life you are in. That can be hard to accept, but as you face
your fears you can move forward.

Worry won't solve the problem. It wears you down and keeps
you from working a solution. I had to work with my set back and get
passed worrying and fearing. Fear kills so let's be fearless and brave.

Think Solution, Not Problem

When you are singing and come across a problem, you want to
think of a solution. Usually what we do instinctively is try to defend
ourselves from impending danger, or worry about it. Your thoughts
need to be on the things that will help you solve the problem, such as
thinking of the sound coming off the roof of your mouth, or taking
a long breath instead of a quick fearful one, so that you have enough
air to complete the phrase. If you have things to draw from in your

"bag of tricks" (vocal technique), then you need to start accessing them so that you're in solution mode. Otherwise, the problem gets bigger, not solved, and you are busy concentrating on the problem instead of fixing it.

After a Mistake in the Song, Go Forward

If you made a mistake, or worse, you broke on a note, it can be hard to recover. Remember when ballplayers miss a shot or lose the ball? They don't stand there; they grab the ball and move forward to finish the game or inning. Going forward can be hard to do but take a breath. A breath is a new adjustment of the muscles, and that means a new beginning. Then, be determined to make the rest of the song the best you can. Think of the technical part of your singing and not the emotional. Doing this keeps you steady until you get the momentum to let go and get past, just like in life itself. As Oswald Chambers said, *"Never let the sense of failure defeat your next step."*

Your Brain Can Be the Enemy

Obstacles are to be dealt with not feared.

Sometimes the voice wants to go higher than the brain allows it to go. It tells you to stop; you might hurt yourself. It says that you don't sound good, so you shouldn't go up any further when exercising. What you have to do is *tell the brain to shut up*. The mind needs to learn to use the tools that you have come to know to improve your sound. It isn't whether or not it doesn't sound good or feels too high; it is whether you will try to help yourself get the notes by accessing what you have learned. You don't want to give into your mental criticism and in doing so, get stuck and stop trying. Usually, if the brain is talking, it isn't good. Very rarely is your mind saying, "Oh you hit that note... great." When it does, be very grateful.

One of my students had performed the first act in the shows we do every six months. While we were backstage getting ready for act 2, she freaked out worrying about her song. She didn't want to go on, fearing she couldn't hit the notes. I told her my story about how I cracked. I had to decide on the next show if I would go for it and believe I could get it, or chicken out and not be determined to do it. (I will share this story later.) I said, "You have to do it or you won't ever try to sing anything hard again. You will regret not going for it, not knowing if you could have done it." She gathered herself as she listened, and as she entered the stage, we looked at each other. With a nod of assurance, she went out and nailed it. This moment will never be forgotten. It will serve her in situations where she will go for it and stand firm with conviction. I am so proud of her. Keep remembering: obstacles are to be dealt with not feared.

When you're going for a high note, are you experiencing a lot of interference? "That note is too high," "my voice sounds so bad," "hope I can make it," "I'm never gonna make that note," etc. Any or all of these thoughts can run through your mind in seconds and do nothing to help you get the note. It does everything to keep you from letting your muscles respond, grow and reach the notes you want to get. Remember this is a tape playing. We don't use tapes anymore! Again, you have to throw the tape away; you have to tell your brain to "shut up!" Immediately think of specific things to help you get that note, sound better, and be confident. Then, go out and nail that note with no thought. Go out and do it.

Perseverance When You Practice and Sing

There will be times your voice isn't responding and you have a hard time with notes or phrases in songs. Your voice may need more warming up at this time, or a mental adjustment on what your focus is. You may be stressed about life, so you're distracted. Work through it. Don't get discouraged. Your voice changes day to day, but if you are consistent with exercising your vocal muscles, warming up before singing, and go over the weak spots in songs, you will bounce back. If you keep having the same problem again and again as you practice a song or a specific part, take it to its least common denominator.

An example of this is trying to hit the high note in a song. Take the note before it and play that note and then the note you are trying to get. By isolating these notes and practicing the jump from one to the other, you are getting your ear used to it and the muscles as well.

You can also go from vowel to vowel instead of word to word. You ride on the vowels and close on consonants. There was a case where we had "u" as in the word "to," going to "a" as in the word "play." My student constantly sang the word play flat, so we had to take it apart to know what would be helpful for him to correct the problem. He sang the vowels on the pitches and changed the formation of his mouth. It worked.

- Establish the interval and have it played while you listen to it. Close your eyes and listen.
- Sing the interval on one vowel first, then the other vowel involved.
- Notice your mouth. Are your teeth closing as you go for the high note? Work on keeping an opening between the teeth.
- If your jaw is coming forward, then keep it back.
- Are you dropping the jaw as you go for the high note? You may be dropping it when you don't need to. You want the mouth open but suddenly dropping the jaw excessively can cause you to sing the pitch off. How does the sound travel out? You want the sound to leave as if it were touching and traveling off the roof of your mouth. If you drop the jaw excessively, you may be pulling down and not allowing the sound to travel out high off the roof. Also, you may be

closing off the back of the throat. Analyzing during practice will allow you to perform without thought and naturally.

Be Confident Around Stars

Stars are only people that have a little or a lot more visibility than you, so don't put them on a pedestal. They need people to be real around them. You may be just as good or better, so believe in yourself. Be confident and be yourself.

There was a party, and John Travolta was celebrating the finishing of one of his early movies. It was a great time for him, but he had too much to drink and came on stage while I was performing with a band. I had to escort him off. The band leader was stunned that I did this; Mr. Travolta was very nice about it.

> *"Success makes life easier. It doesn't make living easier" – Bruce Springsteen*

Fame Won and Lost

The pressure on you if you have fame is enormous. The spotlight is always on you, your family, friends, and all you do. For some, this is what they live for. Some endure it, and others handle it beautifully. It comes too quickly to many young stars, and we see their lives fall to pieces. Many are carried to their ruin by drugs or alcohol. You may have been a child star, the cutest thing since sliced bread. Now you can't get a job. Youth is the calling card; someone tells you, you are too old. Your time in the spotlight has dried up. You find the friends that hung around are no longer there. They don't seem to know you anymore and your troubles are your only companions. You may be looking at all your achievements as the past, and can't find meaning for your future. All of who you are now feels like nothing because it is wrapped up in what was. Bitterness, envy, resentment can settle in.

My dear sweet friends, I know how it feels and how painful the business can be – life too. We must know who we are outside of what we do. That is what keeps us together. Knowing this before, during and after success will keep your mind, heart, and spirit strong through all the seasons. What you do should fulfill you but it cannot be all-consuming, or it will consume you.

Singing and Performing

Finding a song is like trying on clothes.
*You have to try it on to see if it fits **you**.*

Talent needs to be used, so don't hide yours away. I did it for many years - it's no fun. Now I am happy to say I've been brave, blossoming, and learning to be successful. Let's do it together!

When you are looking for a song to sing, most people like the rhythm so much they don't take into account what it's about. With some songs it won't matter, but on the other hand, you are saying these words. You will be conveying what the message of the song is. Go over the words and see if they fit who you are. Sometimes I have a student change some of the words, and then the song will be appropriate for them. This happens if the person is young and the lyrics are too explicit. Just a few changes here and there and voila it fits.

Always *tell the story* when you are singing a song. What is the song about and are you getting that across to the audience? It will make all the difference in the world to you being great or just okay, maybe even really good, but not great.

Learning a Song

A song can be learned many different ways. If you are going to be free to express what the song means to you and get that across to the audience, you need to have several things out of the way first.

- Read so you are aware of the story behind what you are singing.
- Sing the song through.
- Memorize the words.

- Make sure you know the breathing spots.
- Choose the key - What key do you sing in? No such thing. What key do you sing that specific song in is the question.

The Key of the Song

The key of a song can make or break your performance as I experienced while in High School. Don't just accept that you have to sing a song as it comes to you unless these are the conditions you have to deal with as I did.

> *The key of a song can make or break your performance.*

Here's a story about just that...

Bonner High School was the boys' counterpart for Prendergast, where I went to high school. I auditioned for their Musical as a freshman and got two solos and the award for best singer. The next year I got a lead part and best actress award. After that year, I got the lead. I was Tessie Trundle in "How to Make Movies Without Taking Pictures." I loved being on stage and acting as we practiced. But one solo was so high that I really had a hard time singing it. There was no changing the key; you had to sing it where it was. We practiced and practiced and by the time the show came around my voice had had it. The show was going great even though I was hoarse. I knew my voice was almost gone when it came to the song, but I pushed through until coming to a specific part. My voice gave way. Even though I felt bad, I was grateful because somehow there was enough voice left to finish the show. I received the award for best actress, but they said they were disappointed with my singing. What I didn't know to do then, because I couldn't change the key, was to sing the note very light during practice. My voice wouldn't have been so tired and I could have gotten the note in the performance.

Exceptions to being able to choose a key are Classical and Musical Theatre pieces. There you must sing them as they are written. Someone may have a song and all the music is set – there too, you have to sing the song in that key. These are times when you must use all your skills to master any trouble spots. You may have to lighten up before a high note that wouldn't shine otherwise. You may need to take a bigger breath or use even more support than usual for the note or part that is challenging. No matter what, you have to make it work.

In all other instances:

- It is a myth to say you sing in a particular key. You may sing a certain genre of music in the same key, but that is because most of that music is centered around the same melody or chord structure, like the blues.
- Try at least three keys up or down to see what best suits your voice. Sometimes you don't have to go that far to find the key that suits you, but always be open to trying another key. You sing the song where it is best for you.
- Don't think you have to sing the song where an artist recorded it. You have to consider your instrument and sing it where you feel most comfortable. Sing it where it will bring out the best in your instrument, *your* voice.

Running Out of Air in a Song

Running out of air, especially in a long phrase can happen because of a variety of bad habits.

- Check if you are throwing some of your air out before you start the first word. You aren't starting with support (outwardness) but pulling down with the rib cage. Recording yourself, or just being mindful to listen as you are singing will reveal if this is your problem.

- Put your hand close to your mouth when you sing. You shouldn't feel a lot of air hitting your hand.
- Check with a mirror to see if you are lifting the shoulders while taking a breath, and then going down when you start to sing. What comes up must come down - your shoulders. You will have taken in air but you also caused tightness and tension. And even though you took air in, now you can't access all of it because of that tension.
- At the beginning of a long phrase, approach it with less volume, then you will be able to sing it through.
- Make sure the rib cage is up and forward even though you are running out of air at the end of sentences.

Tetrazzini, a great opera singer of the past, mentioned that you should think of the air leaving against the chest. You can't do that if you pull down so keep the chest and body up and chest forward. Be up; don't pull up as you take a breath.

Vibrato

Vibrato adds quality to your tone. Many have a hard time bringing out vibrato when holding a note, or need help learning how to make it happen. Even a teacher at Musicians Institute

> *Vibrato adds quality to your tone.*

wasn't sure how to teach this and asked me how I explained it to my students. It is made in the laryngeal area, not by the abdominal area. If you shake in the abdominal area for vibrato, then you take away your ability to support your tones. Let's look at some ways you can try to make vibrato happen.

- Hold a comfortable tone, but don't increase your volume, just hold it. Think of your throat as being held open very wide. At the very end, if you are able to stay open, the vibrato will start. You might hear only a slight movement but be patient and it will come. There should be no movement in the abdominal area. Put your hand there to check.

• Wave your hand in front of you and follow the up and down movement as you hold a comfortable note. I know this seems silly, and my students and I laugh at it also, but it can help, try it!

• Hit a comfortable note on the piano and then the note next to it (a semitone), you slowly increase the movement from one to the other as your voice follows. Increase the speed until you get the movement in your voice to go fast. Wave your hand really fast to follow the movement up and down of each note. You are seeing and hearing the movement to help your vocal folds follow and start the vibrato.

Do Not Attack the Attack

The attack is the beginning of the phrase when you start singing, or it's the beginning sound you make. Some start their sound with a rough, guttural beginning, or a tightening of muscles. When you enter singing like this you're banging the vocal folds together. This practice done over and over again can cause damage. If this is your habit you need to work on changing how you enter into the attack.

Try using a silent "h" as you go to sing. It is as if you are landing a plane. You don't jam the front down and smack the landing - you will have a lot of lawsuits… Hmmm. You want a smooth landing and that's the same with your attack - make a smooth landing. Think of air flowing through with your sound.

As you enter the beginning of the phrase or song, you also should have your mouth ready for that sound/pitch and think of it mentally. This helps you hit the center of the tone which is going to be invaluable when you're recording as well as live performing.

When you start to sing, just after taking in air, there can be a tendency to drop the rib cage, thus causing the abdominals to tighten - the crunch. Just like when you are doing crunches in the gym these muscles are tightened, but for singing, you want to keep the rib cage up, so you don't do - the crunch.

- Keep the ribs lifted.
- Abs in tonus (in use) but not overly tensed like a hard ball. The definition of tonus is: the constant low-level activity of a body tissue, especially muscle tone. Another definition is: a normal state of continuous slight tension in muscle tissue that facilitates its response to stimulation. So you want the muscle to be working but not feeling it too tight (tensed).

Don't Throw Away the Last Words of the Sentences

Sometimes these words get lost. Maybe it's because you are so intent on getting to the next phrase or concerned with getting enough air in for it, that you cut the last word of your sentence short. Maybe you just have a habit of dropping your voice there. Whatever the cause, try to finish the last words of sentences to get the full meaning of what you are singing, or saying for that matter. Have them be heard and flow naturally.

Do Keep the Mouth Open to Finish the Last Word When Speaking

With speaking and in voice therapy it is a given that we have to work on this. Check the very end syllable of the last word; you will be surprised at how low it goes. By being aware of this you can practice keeping your voice up and your mouth open. Sometimes the sound is so soft that you can't be heard.

Do Not - let the audience know you made a mistake unless you can make it a part of the show. They don't need to worry about you. They are there to be entertained. Let it go. You are there to give to them all you got - so do just that. When you get backstage and out of earshot, then you can scream and shout about your boo-boo.

Do Open Your Mouth

You think your mouth is open but if you look at so many singers singing high and loud, you will realize you need to open it even more. This may be out of many singers comfort zone. The proof is in the pudding. See if this helps you:

- Press your thumb and forefinger together, put them between your side teeth and make sure your nails fit in that opening.
- Notice your top teeth, not only in the front but the sides also.
- Do not drop your jaw anymore but widen your mouth. I know this is contrary to many teachings but try it.
- The lower lip should be in an oval shape not squared (pulled down on the sides and thus tensed), nor pulled inward causing tension in the jaw muscles. It should look as it does when you smile. When you laugh the lower lip is usually relaxed so copy that.
- If the jaw starts to come forward, put your tongue on top of your bottom teeth, but don't bring your tongue out any further. The jaw is usually too active and this helps it to be relaxed.

Dry Mouth

If you have a dry mouth, bite the tip of your tongue.

If you have dry mouth, bite the tip of your tongue.

This will bring saliva into the mouth when you feel dry. If you can turn around for a few seconds, do the tongue rotation and tongue press as this will start circulation. Also be mindful to take lots of air in as you breathe going forward.

Remembering Words

Make sure you go over the first line of your song before entering the stage. So many of us have gone out and the beginning line is nowhere to be found in our memory. You may have sung the song many times but for some reason you just blitzed on the beginning. Always say your beginning line backstage if you are singing one song. If you are doing a show, lots of songs, then do it for all of them.

Another aid with words in the song and getting notes is using a hand gesture. One of my students was making the same mistake of chopping a sentence and then ending on a wrong note. She had to audition the next day. I told her to move both arms slowly outward as she sang the line, remembering to deliver it smoothly with the arms as they moved across her body. Then, she was to put her hand out twice for the note she needed to repeat. She never made the mistake again but had to practice a little more with the arms and being smooth with her sentence. It works!

Swallowing the Tone

If you pull the muscles of the throat down too much, you may make your sound seem swallowed. It is made too far back in the throat. Think of the sound coming from the roof of the mouth and aim for the middle of the roof as you are bringing your sound out of the mouth. Make sure the tongue is forward and touching the bottom teeth. Also, think of the sound coming forward as it leaves your mouth. Direct your focus on the sound leaving as if high on the face around the base of the cheek bones or higher. As you go for higher notes, think of them leaving as if your skull is lifting in the center.

Mouth Alive

When you are singing, your mouth and interior of the mouth is the last stage of your sound leaving the body. It helps bring forth your sound. If the cheekbones are down, the sides of the lips are pulled down, or the teeth closed, your sound won't carry very far. You can still sing like this, and if this is your style, then that is the choice you are making to convey your singing. No matter what style though, when you want to grow your muscles, convey excitement, hit high or hard notes, you need a mouth that is alive with your sound.

- Open your mouth, not too long but wide.
- See the top side teeth.
- Lift the cheekbones.
- Make sure the sides of your lips are facing upwards.
- Keep the tongue flat and from sliding back too far.
- Make sure you can see in the back of the mouth (if you're holding vowels other than "ee" as in the word see.)
- Smile!

Projecting

Think of the sound traveling out far from you, as well as widening as it travels, like a horn in a speaker. It is narrow in the back and widens at the end. Keep the thought of your sound widening and going forward as the notes and words leave your body. Your sound will travel farther and have more volume. The production of your sound and pitch accuracy plays a vital part in the resonance also.

Looking at the Audience

When you are singing or speaking, don't look your audience in the eye unless you are very confident. You have to be ready to see all kinds of expressions and not let it throw you off. People don't know how their facial expressions look, and if they did, they would probably change them. Their faces don't always portray what they think of your performance. Some faces are set in a frown. Some are off thinking of the day, or the appointment they have to keep. What if they are texting! If you look at the top of their head, their hair, that is just the same to them as if you are looking them in the eye. This will get you the comfort you need to communicate the song to your audience, and not get thrown off. Little by little you can work on looking straight at individuals in the audience. But always - Smile!

What Hand Holds the Mic?

The hand that talks, gives direction, and is going to give more expression is the hand you write with. Hold the mic with the other hand. Most people limit themselves here. Of course you can switch hands and should, but for the majority of the time keep your writing hand free.

Why Is It That Some Days I Can Hit Notes and Other Days I Can't?

First, your voice is part of all you experience each day and changes depending upon what happens. If you are tired, you affect the voice. When you have an upset, are sick, or just have a bad day, these and just life in general can make a difference in your voice. It is part of your body and has nerve endings, muscles, cartilages, etc. involved. This is why you have to check to see where your voice is at for that day. Then you have to work around what you have. Keep positive.

A singer came to me and said he starts to sing and it sounds bad, then in a little while, the voice sounds good, and then the voice tires. I asked some questions and explained that if he warmed his voice up and did some strengthening, he would see better results and consistency from his voice. After you've been practicing and building your muscular strength, there will be a consistency your voice will give you. You can count on this consistency and level of performance, unless something unforeseen happens, like a sickness that affects the voice. Muscles will work but not as well as if you took the time to do a few exercises to warm them up. I have to remind myself to stop and warm up my voice before practicing a song. I always remember before performing, but just going over some songs seems so easy, and why take the time - wrong, it matters.

Growth

Growth is not always a steady march forward. You will experience a lot of times when you wonder why your voice isn't getting better or even may be a little less than the week before. Through these times you will get frustrated and wonder why you ever started, but this is why - to learn.

Work through these times and your voice will come out even better. These dips in progress are normal, so fight through and you will pass through them in a very short time, just like life.

Stage Fright

If you are shaking before a performance, you're alive. Sometimes that nervousness gets to be overwhelming

Fears are meant to be faced, or they never go away.

139

though. Try taking long breaths and thinking of your muscles in the shoulders coming down as you arch the back and lift the chest to an erect stature. Next, concentrate on breathing in through the nose and out the mouth. Think about parts of the song and how you will go for notes, how you will breathe and then support those notes. Think of where you will move on a specific part of the song. As you concentrate on things you will do, your brain doesn't have as much hold on thoughts that make you nervous. You then need to believe you can do it as you have prepared and are ready. Keep breathing in confidence and *all* distractions out.

Sing for only one person, then two, then more and more. Make the setting as comfortable as possible as you work on your stage fright. Try sitting when you sing, as you can feel more grounded then. The most important thing is that you don't give up. Use the nervousness to your advantage and be ready to take all that energy to good use on stage. Let it lift you not control you. Backstage is a time for steadying yourself. What is your fright? Do you think you won't remember the words? Do you feel naked in front of all those people? Did something happen in a song and you are afraid it will keep happening, like losing your voice or not making a note? (I can relate.) I know it seems like a simple answer, but practice is more often than not, the solution. You must practice the way that will give you results and calm your fears. Fears are meant to be faced or they never go away. Start believing in yourself, practice, and face your fears.

Stress

Being a little stressed about performing is helpful in that you have an edge going. You're pumped and want to get out there. It is when you aren't using it in a positive way that stress can pull you back instead of forward. That adrenalin before singing can keep you on your toes and ready to do a great performance. When on stage, you need to be a little bigger than life, so that stress (being pumped) can propel you to that stature. "I'm stressed about the show" can equal, "I want to do a great job," or "I'm gonna give it my all." The secret to a great show is lots of practice. Know the words, and what you plan to do really well. It eases the stress of not being prepared. You can easily overcome this. Just practice more than you want, be ready and use that stress to your advantage.

On the other hand, stress from life can throw you off your game. You must leave all the stresses of life out of your mind if you want to perform. They don't belong or must not be carried with you on stage. Even when you practice you have to let them go. Easier said than done right? I know, but you must be strong and deal with them or they will deal with you. They keep you from being your best in life and your art.

Trauma

If you have experienced trauma in your life, it may be hard to overcome but you can, as so many of us have had to do. I hope my sharing this next experience and working through it will give you hope with what *you* have to deal with.

In 1999 I Had an Accident that almost ended my singing. I had a habit of taking dogs in, getting them shots, fixed, and ready for a home that I would find. Neighbors told me about a dog that was in our complex for two months, and no one would take her in. When I found homes for the last female and her pups that I rescued, I took her in. She was a pit bull mix and very loving, but my girl Nova (Nova is a dog, but still my girl), didn't want anyone else here in our home. My boy Tiger, (pit and rot), was ready to fight at the drop of a hat. Well, Peaceful (that was her name), got out of the kitchen where she was, came upstairs to my office where my dogs and I were, and was ready to attack Nova. I turned around and put my arm out

141

to take her back downstairs. She got me instead of Nova. I couldn't do anything to stop her and get her to let go of my wrist. I was like a rag doll she was tossing around. Over and over again she shook my wrist. There was blood everywhere. I called her name, but she had gone red, meaning after taking the first bite, pits are locked in and don't respond. Finally, she started to stand still but wouldn't let go, and my dog Tiger, after two other attempts, came and attacked her. In so doing, she let go of me. I got away, but my boy was in the room fighting. After three tries I got them to stop and separated them. I had lost a lot of blood, but as usual, I thought I could handle it... Hmmm. A student came for a lesson and found me very weak. Imagine coming for a lesson and seeing your teacher with blood covering her arm. I can't remember if I called my friend or his mother did, but my friend Roger came and took me to the hospital. I had no insurance, so I was taken by ambulance to another hospital where I waited in the emergency room on a gurney. They didn't want to do anything there with local anesthesia, so I was admitted, given painkillers and waited a day and a half. In the middle of the night, I was awakened and told I was going into surgery.

When I woke up the next day, I was hoarse. The nurse told me it would go away. The doctor told me it would go away. After a month, it didn't go away. My youngest sister, Mariette referred me to an excellent doctor, *Dr. Kantor* in Beverly Hills. Upon leaving his office, I almost fainted from the news he posed. He showed me a video of my vocal folds that had this large mass blocking 40% of my air passage. When I was in the hospital and was intubated, they nicked my vocal folds causing this mass. It wasn't going away, and Dr. Kantor said that if it was attached on both sides of the vocal folds, they would have to cut my thyroid cartilage in half from the outside. I would never sing again. If it was attached on one side, he could remove it and I would be fine.

My life was before me, and I was devastated. What would I do? Would I lose my home eventually, and my animals? Where would I go that I could keep them if I couldn't make a living? It was already getting hard to breath. I stopped teaching. A month later after trying acupuncture and herbs, I took the chance with surgery by Dr. Kantor to remove the mass. What a relief, it was attached on one side. The doctor's orders were to not talk for a week. Dr. Kantor said everything was fine, and I could start to sing, but I wasn't fine at all. I was scared. My voice was weak and what if I hurt it by straining. It took years to get over this trauma. I wasn't the same for so long. It did bring me to sing with more knowledge and forethought. There is always something you can glean from your situation. Maybe you have gone through a trauma and have vocal problems where your voice is weak. I am here to tell you - *you* can overcome.

The voice is resilient, and that is what *we* have to be. Don't give in to your fears as they will want to surround you with doubt. Find a good voice therapist and work your voice back to health. You may have to change some habits or find a different way to approach your songs, but you can do it. Have faith and work your butt off. You are worth it. There is no one else that can give what you have to offer.

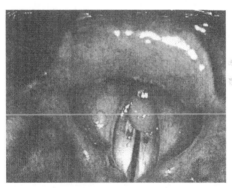

Growth caused by surgery August 28, 1999

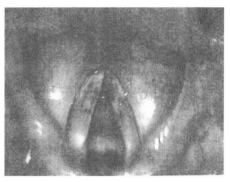

After surgery November 9, 1999
Surgery performed by Dr. Edward A. Kantor

Don't analyze...go for it!

Going After Notes

Our brains are such tricky things. They speak and analyze as we go through our daily tasks. Check your mental talk. It may be criticizing and holding you in "analysis paralysis." Anu Gunn used this term when we were getting him ready to record and it is perfect to use here.

When going for a note, don't hesitate, it breaks your momentum. There is a time for pondering on *how* you go after a note, but in the midst of when you are going for it, don't analyze - go. Momentum can't be stopped at the last minute, or you lose the follow-through necessary to make that note.

Work not worry – If you worry about going for a note, you are busy and held back from doing what will help you get it. Pull your mind to what will help - the things you have learned. Then, go for it and trust.

144

Higher Notes and Your Focus

Focus on remembering that you are resonating with a shorter resonating area when making higher sounds. Think from the mandible (jaw - between your teeth) up when bringing forth your sound. Even with lower notes, you need to keep this in mind.

What is your attitude toward the note? If you think it is unattainable, it will be. It cannot be thought of as reaching to a mountaintop. Don't look up to the top and see the note there. It will scare you. You will think it's too high and hard to reach. Think it is in front of you and attainable. You must be mentally strong and determined to get that note.

Bad Habits

If you have bad habits and still want to keep them, like some rasp in your voice, that is your choice. If you strengthen the muscles enough, they will stand a certain amount, which you have to be aware and respectful of, but no more. The biggest thing is to heal if you are injured, strengthen, and use wisdom.

Courage is resistance to fear, mastery of
fear, not absence of fear -Mark Twain

Marquita as Mother Teresa

"VISIONS" a Rock Opera

While doing a rock opera and playing the part of Mother Teresa, I cracked! Her words were made into a song by Dimitris Papakostas (who goes by the name "D's" now) for his Rock Opera "Visions." It was very challenging. All the singers were so good and seemed to have no problem singing their prospective songs. On the other hand, I had several parts in the song that challenged my voice because they were in the area referred to as the break. Each time I had to do my song I was fearful of missing a particular note. On the second preview night of the opening, I did just that... I cracked. How embarrassing, and to top it off, the producer and music director called me on stage in front of the whole cast after the performance that night. They asked me to sing a lower note so that I wouldn't repeat the same crack for the sake of the show.

The next day I had the formal opening night to face. I couldn't find another note that would sound anywhere near as good, and it would be lower, killing this high point in the song. I called my sister Melody and cried. She had never heard me crack. I poured out my heart to God. In prayer, I asked Him to help me know what to do. Then I proceeded to continue beating myself up mentally. Sound familiar? I knew everyone would be listening backstage, as well as the audience, to see what I would do. That evening as I was going on, dressed in my Mother Teresa costume and rosary beads, I stood in the wings, waiting and praying. "Lord, this is it. If I don't go for it, I'll never be the same. The producers could fire me if I croak again, not to mention the embarrassment - again. But I have to go for it Lord, please help me." That was it; I was going for it no matter what. I went on stage and sang through the song trying not to think of what would happen. Then I came to the breath before. I took it – YES - got the note! From that point on I never looked back. I knew I could do it. Even though fear would start, I did it each time from then on. I didn't listen or give in to the fear. I faced it.

It will be your turn. Maybe it's now when a difficulty is happening and challenging you. You will need to muster up faith in yourself. See yourself nailing it and not looking back. There may be a technical problem. No matter what, you can overcome it if you want to.

Talent hidden makes no one happy - be
brave. Let's make smiles happen

Sing-Sing-Sing

If you say you're a runner, you need to be running. If you say you're a speaker, you need to get out and speak, or write, or whatever you claim you do. Be active, be doing it. So if you say you sing, then get out and sing. I don't care where. Nothing takes the place of singing your songs for the muscles to become familiar with them and used to responding to the notes you want to hit. This lets you free to express the meaning of the song. Again, there is only one of you, so you are needed to give what only you can give... start singing!

Be the Best You Can Be

What you do is a gift to the audience receiving it, so you want to make it the best you can. Aim for the top in your quality. Don't accept mediocrity. Just being okay at your

> *Enjoy the fact you are doing what you Love.*

craft isn't enough. Excellence is what you want to strive for. Fears will come. Center on being the best you can be. Enjoy the fact you are doing what you *LOVE*.

Whatever You Have, Use It

I thought it was over if I reached 26 or 27 years old. That is what I told myself when I was in my 20's. Is the clock ticking and you feel you're too old to start or have a career? As a matter of fact, a guy from my old neighborhood called me a "has been!" And that was decades ago when this person unwittingly set me into a deep questioning of myself. Luckily I decided to disregard his assumption and keep doing what *I love*. At 71 years old and counting, I am still singing and have been teaching for decades. I love what I do and know I wouldn't be a happy person suppressing my talents, and you won't be either. Keep doing what *YOU LOVE.* You will make this world a happier place for so many and yourself.

Perform Regularly

You have to be used to being in front of an audience for timing and delivery as well as muscle memory. Performing regularly takes the edge off. You get used to being under the gun. That becomes the norm.

The mountains we have built in our minds
keep us from climbing the hills they are.

Visualizing

Believing You Can Do It

I want you to concentrate on seeing yourself singing. See yourself enjoying going for the high notes. No straining, just going for the note and it is easy. See the audience. You are so happy to be there giving your gift to them. Can you do this? If not, you need to. Keep working on it. See yourself being successful. So many books are written on the subject of success and what you can do to attain it. Start reading them because they will inspire you as they have me. See yourself hitting all the notes that you fear. We all have areas in songs that challenge us. Think of exactly what you have to do to get that note. See the soft palate lift. And think of how the note will travel through, past the back of the throat and out. See the ribs expanding to take the breath before any sentence where you usually forget to take a breath, or where you don't take enough breath. Mentally practice going over these areas and being able to sing with ease.

Before going on stage, see yourself entering and how you will smile and greet the audience, no matter what your eyes fall on. You are focused on being successful and giving the best. Remember the audience wants you to succeed.

When you're recording keep focused on the intent of the song and what you want to convey through your voice. You have to already have gone over the technical part beforehand. Now you are, interested and focused on your feelings. See an audience in your mind. Sing to them. Their ears will hear that feeling.

In one of *Norman Vincent Peale's* books, "Positive Imaging," he wrote about a man who gave his story at a luncheon. He had come to Hong Kong with his wife and eight children from Red China. They had nothing, just the clothes they were wearing and what little they carried. He kept believing the scripture verse, "I can do all things through Christ who strengthens me." He applied it to his life and worked very hard. He imaged himself going from poverty to being a very successful businessman. This is what this man thought, worked hard at, and told others. He believed he could and decided he would. He followed through with doing and became very successful.

Believe, work hard and you will do it!

Throw the Negative Tapes Out

Sometimes we are the worst enemy we can have. We tell ourselves how bad we are at what we do. Then, when we go to progress and move forward, our brain scolds us with all these past statements like: "That was terrible!" "You can't hit that note." "You're too old to do that." "You're a has-been!" "You're too overweight to be signed!" Etcetera. The list is endless, and you acquiesce to the commander-in-chief, your brain. Replace these thoughts with an antidote such as: "That was terrible" changed to "I am getting better at that." "You can't hit that note" changed to "I am going after that note, and I will hit it with practice." "You're too old to do that" changed to "You are never too old to do what you *Love*," and so forth. This is honest and forthright. Keep dousing the negative until the positive comes streaming out of your mind. It may take some time, but you can do it. Don't give up, keep changing these thoughts and you will begin to be the positive statements you are saying.

Goal Setting

Make Your Goal a Reality Day By Day

Do something toward your goal every day. I know many people say this and it is so true. I procrastinated doing this book for decades because I gave myself the excuse that today, I had something else that needed to be done. "The emergency of the moment" became more important than what I needed to do, which was finishing this book.

- First make a goal. If you don't make a goal you have nowhere to aim to or for. I tell my students we are aiming for the top and nothing less. Then no matter what, our standard is high.
- Write down the night before what and when you will do something towards that goal for the next day.
- Make a weekly plan and review each day's agenda just in case you need to reschedule something. Keeping to your plan ensures that you get what you need to do accomplished. I find that if I don't plan to do a specific thing, then I find little things to do and never get to the work that will bring me closer to achieving my goal.
- Do not do busy work. Every time I used to start having trouble finding the thoughts to write for this book, the equipment didn't work for recording, or I couldn't seem to solve a problem, I wanted to do something around the house. There went an hour. Sometimes I didn't even go back to what I was doing. Taking a break during work is necessary but in these instances it was me copping out. If you resonate with this then try to stay just a little longer each time and fight through the urge to give up.
- Make your goal time an appointment. We make appointments for doctors and other things and we usually don't miss those or reschedule them. For me this was magic.

- Find a room, put a do not disturb sign on it and close the door. Let the family know how important it is for you to do work on your goals during this time.
- Be accountable to someone for doing a specific amount of work and when you will have it done. Having that check helps you to go forward and could be the difference between finishing it through or not.

In 2010 I decided to make sure I got the songs for my second Album written. I told several people that I was writing a song a month and I did. I kept reminding myself of two things. First, I made a promise to myself and God to do these Christian songs and second I told others what I was going to do. How lame it would be if I didn't do what I said I was going to do. That worked. I finished all the songs and on time.

I am reminded of these and other driving forces for success by my mentor *Darren Hardy*, in his "Insane Productivity Program." He has made me aware of a whole new level of commitment and achievement. I now get up earlier than ever before to make sure there is enough time to do my priorities. I do my priorities (appointments) with no distractions like my cell phone ringing or notifying me when someone sent a text. Emails are nonexistent during this time.

There is so much I have and continue to learn from Darren. He interviewed *Tim Grover*, the coach for many athletes such as Michael Jordan, Kobe Bryant, and many others. Tim Grover talked about being "Relentless," the name of his book (which I immediately went out and got as well as "Compound Effect" written by Darren Hardy.) These men are game changers if you want to achieve your goals. One bottom line they both stress is hard work but it is worth it.

Breathing and the Act of Singing

We singers use our voices over a wide range and need to take special care of our voices, but actors, preachers, lecturers, teachers, voice users of all types, need to have the skills which will keep their voices healthy and useful also.

Take a deep breath. I can take a deep breath in many different and possibly wrong ways. How do I take a breath so that my notes soar, that is the question. You are the instrument and player. That means you have to take more care in your breathing habits, as well as many other aspects of how you approach your voice. The reward you receive will be well worth it in the long run.

Breath

Every breath brings readjustment for your muscles, opportunity to throw off tension, and preparation for a vocal achievement.

Breathe with the tempo of the song.

Breathe with the tempo of the song. If the song is slow, then the breath you take is slow. If it is fast then the breath is fast. Each breath should have its note equivalent in your mind. Sometimes we think there is no time for a breath when there is. By giving the breath a note value, a place in time, you will relax enough to be able to fit it in. It also helps when you have a tendency to forget to breathe.

Breathe - Take More Breaths - Mark You're Breathing Points

I like to be comfortable when I sing. I tell my students to take more breaths. Sometimes we want to challenge ourselves, and see if we can make it through a long phrase without taking a breath.

That's okay, but only if you can do this without compromising your abilities to support the phrase. Usually, I see people struggling and then pushing to make it towards the end. Why? Just take another breath. You may be pleasantly surprised that you can sing the phrase a lot better. Also you will have enough air at the end to hold a note you otherwise would have to cut off. You were out of air, and out of options. Taking a breath where you usually wouldn't, can change the texture of the phrase, and cause more variety in your style.

When you breathe before you sing, don't stop and pause. It is, breathe - sing, not breathe ----- sing. Think of a sneeze. Your body forces you to take a breath whether you like it or not. So don't separate your breath from when you start to sing or speak. Pausing between thoughts when talking is a spot to be careful of. A lot of time we forget to breathe there.

Straw Breath

Some of my students, when breathing, look as if they are breathing in through a straw. You don't get as much air as you need for singing. It also creates tension in the laryngeal area. The mouth shouldn't change to a closed position to take a breath. Practice looking in the mirror to make sure you are keeping your mouth open as you breathe. It's just like speaking. You don't close your mouth or breathe through the nose when you talk. So it is with singing. Breathe through the mouth and keep the mouth open as you breathe.

The Function of Breathing

You are dealing with sets of muscles. Working them in the right way can bring you results very quickly. Here is an overview of their function.

The function of breathing is one that we do without thinking. Just take note right now how you are taking air in, this is called inhalation, and how you are leaving air out, exhalation. It's something that needs no forethought and is done rather quickly. Singing is a *secondary act* on the function of breathing. You are using the same muscles but in a slightly different way. When you inhale, the *inhalation muscles* are coming into tension, causing the *rib cage* to expand. The *diaphragm*, which some refer to as the breathing muscle, is the floor of the lungs. It flattens allowing the chest cavity to fill when taking in air. When you exhale, the inhalation muscles relax, as the *exhalation muscles* are pulling the ribs back, down, and pressing in. The diaphragm goes back to its original relaxed position, which is dome-like, when air has left the lungs. With the act of singing, when you inhale you will usually take in more air while expanding the ribs, flattening the diaphragm, and filling the chest cavity. When you exhale you want to keep the rib cage out allowing the diaphragm to go back up slowly, and the chest cavity to deflate slower. This will enable you to use a steady stream of air for singing, as opposed to regular breathing where you just let those muscles relax, causing the air to leave much faster.

There is an area just below where the rib cage comes together in the front of the body (below the end of the *sternum*), which is called the *epigastrium*. In this area and beyond is the *abdominal muscle* running up and down from the fifth, sixth, and seventh ribs, to the pelvic bone. Because of the diaphragm descending into this area as it flattens, making room for and drawing air into the chest cavity (thorax), it pushes this area out. This is what you feel and not the diaphragm when placing your hand in this area. (Also referred to as the *Solar Plexus*.) It is the *action of the diaphragm* you feel, and not the diaphragm itself. You should feel this area coming out in coordination with the rib cage expanding. If allowed the ribs will expand and lift as you breathe. It also brings out the lower abdominal area if it is relaxed.

A lot of singers pull in on the abdominal area. It can be because it is overlooked or sometimes not addressed in learning. It may be the opposite, and you are taught to pull in. Many dancers have a hard time with breathing as they are trained to tighten and pull in the abdominals which makes it harder for them to do the opposite for singing. Also in not wanting to have a "stomach," the abdominal area is held in. The old "pull that stomach in" routine doesn't help this situation. So don't pull in or up, just out.

Though there are many ways we can take in air, we will have rib breathing and belly (abdominal) breathing, working together, giving you the maximum amount of breath and ability of usage for singing. Other types of breathing can be and are used but I believe they have pitfalls and don't give you the maximum amount of breath. You need and deserve the best. As you do the right things you will see the results in your voice, in ease of singing, and ability to express without being restricted by lack of air. The proof is in the pudding.

> *The proof is in the pudding.*

Phrases that might be helpful are: "Sitting on the breath," "Singing on the gesture of inhalation." You are holding the tension of the inhalation muscles to create a holding tank effect so that the air will leave a lot slower.

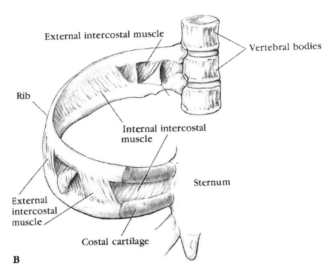

The intercostals muscles between each rib
Image from "Anatomical and Physiological Bases of Speech" by David
R. Dickson and Wilma M. Dickson and used with their permission.

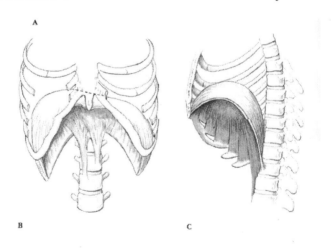

The Diaphragm
Image from "Anatomical and Physiological Bases of Speech" by David
R. Dickson and Wilma M. Dickson and used with their permission.

4-3. *Sagittal section through the head and neck showing the airway (solid line) and food channel (dashed line).*

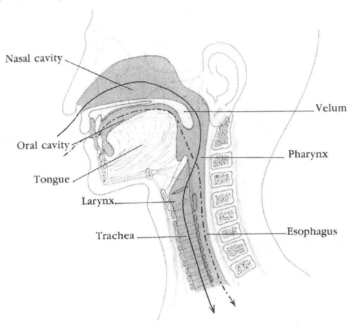

Image from "Anatomical and Physiological Bases of Speech" by David R. Dickson and Wilma M. Dickson and used with their permission.

Consistency towards our craft will pay dividends in the long run.

Breathing Exercises

Your singing is done when and instead of just exhaling air. It is now sound. So remember that inhalation, taking air in, comes before it. Then on bringing air back up to the vocal folds, air causes them to blow apart, vibrate and make sound. You might think this is ridiculous to say, but you'd be surprised at how many of us don't take air in before singing, or take in very little. The rule is:

THINK – BREATHE – SING, not just sing.

Use a mirror to see what is happening as you practice these exercises. The more senses you use, the better your chances of understanding and learning.

"KK" - Know that you Know – If you feel that you are expanding the rib cage and allowing the abdominal area to come out, you may be correct. If you look in a mirror you will see if you are doing it correctly, so "know that you know," use a mirror. Feelings can be right or wrong, but when you see it, you know for sure. If you're a beginner wear something that is form fitting, but not too tight so you can easily look at your body.

Inhalation

Bringing air into the body is inhalation and here are some exercises to help you.

"Sides"

- Make a fist, put your hands on your sides at your rib cage.
- Let all your air out and press your fists in on your sides (ribs).

- As you take the next breath you want to see your fists moving out as you fill with air.
- You want to see and feel the rib cage expand.
- Hold this position (outward) for four beats (approx. 4 seconds).
- You don't want to see the chest being pulled or raised, just expanded. The chest might rise a little, but it will be just a little, and hardly noticeable if noticeable at all.
- Relax the abs but don't pull in, then do the exercise again.

At LACC I interviewed Dr. Abbott, and he said the word expand for the midsection. I know I used that word many times before, but for some reason it gave me a cartoon image of "Expando Man." Kids love it. I remind them of cartoons where someone expanded like a balloon, and they immediately get it.

"Fingertips"

- With the fingertips of both hands together in the front, just below the sternum, and after you've exhaled, press your hands in on the body.
- Take a breath - you should see your fingertips move apart, because the diaphragm descended, causing the abdominal area to be pushed out. You will also see your hands move out on the side, because of the ribs expanding.
- Hold this position (outward) for four beats, (approx. 4 seconds).

Remember: The body movement should be out and expanded not up and long. You should see the sides moving out instead of the chest lifting. This will be confirmed by looking in a mirror - Look!

You don't want to see your body straightening up as if to stand up straight when you start to inhale. As you take the air in, you should already be standing correctly.

Shoulders don't lift. It causes tension and doesn't allow for good intake of air. Also if you lift up, you will probably pull down when you exhale or sing. When you do this it makes the abdominal muscles too tense and can cause the throat muscles to constrict.

If you are slouching, which most of us do, all of the weight of the top of the body is on your midsection. At a point when inhaling you are stopped because of this. Make sure you aren't pressing downward, but are up and forward with the chest. The shoulders are pulled back. Ah, you look great!

Exhalation/Support

Exhalation

Exhalation, leaving air out of the body, is also done when you are singing. You are no longer just breathing. Since you're now singing, you have to support.

Support

Have you ever wanted to add notes and dynamics to your range or wonder why you struggle for some high notes? Are the speeches that used to be easy leaving your voice tired or even gone? Are your auditions going as you would like? Are you beginning to audition and having a problem singing or speaking out? Want to know what to do? The lack of support can be a big reason these things happen.

Support is just an extension of exhalation muscle usage. You stay outward in the abdominal area and when a high and challenging note or passage comes along, you press a little more outward to take the force of that note. You take the force, not only in the front but the back and sides - as if you have a wide belt that you press outward against all the way around. You take the preponderance (weight, power, etc.) of the note downward in the abdominal area and the note flies up and out, an opposing action. Voila, it works!

Think outward from the rib cage as usual but make an extra press outward in the epigastric (the upper central abdominal) region as well as the rib cage. It is an aid most of the time but you still have to have proper development of the vocal muscles. Both the breathing muscles and the vocal muscles must work together and be equally coordinated.

Remember:

- Do not push down with the chest and ribs onto the abdominal area where the ribs come apart or you will tighten and tense, making it more like a crunch you would do in working out. It causes your muscles to lock down, so to speak, instead of allowing the abs to be flexible and outward in their tension. So press outward with the ribs and abs keeping the chest and ribs up and out.
- Keep the back straight. Try not to arch backward or forward and that will do it. If you bend backward, you tighten the abs. Again, it's a similar tension as when you're doing a crunch. You aren't supporting but tensing too much. Bending forward won't give you as much air and leaves you without the ability to sustain or support your notes.

  Truly, you can sing in any position, but this is to practice the best and most beneficial way. So when and if you like or have to put your body in a so-called wrong position, you have the means to go back and practice the way that will keep your voice healthy, and getting the range of notes you want.

Breathiness

If your sound has a lot of air coming out with the tone, then you won't strengthen your muscles as much as you need. Your style is one thing, and there if you like a lot of breath then great, that is your style. But if you're vocalizing and wanting to strengthen your voice, then the breathiness has to be cut back and eliminated. Not enough closure of the vocal folds is one cause of breathiness. Sometimes it is enough for students to imitate my sound, otherwise:

- Press your thumbs together thinking of your vocal folds coming together.

- Look at the picture of the vocal folds making closure in this book. That will bring the idea across of what you have to do.
- A Note of caution - HYPERVENTILATING

If you take in a lot of air and then let it out without supporting you could start to get dizzy – actually, you're hyperventilating. If you start to get dizzy, stop and rethink how to support, but wait until the dizziness leaves or you may just blackout. Here are some ways to learn correct support:

Tension - Relax

- Without breathing or with a little breath, you tense the abdominal area outward to your fist then relax it.
- You shouldn't pull in to relax it. Just let go, or just let it relax by not tensing outward anymore. It is a much smaller movement than if you pull in.

The purpose of this exercise is mainly to show what happens to this area while breathing. The tension part is an example of when you're singing, and the relax part is what must happen before taking your next breath. Air cannot travel if the muscles remain tense. You must relax these muscles before each breath. Otherwise, you will create tension, not be able to take in a good amount of air, and very possibly strain.

Belly Breathing

This exercise I mentioned before is the prep for doing the following exercises, so I am going to explain it again.

- Lie on the floor and put a large book on the abdominal area just above and below the belly button but also below the sternum.
- Inhale and watch to see the book rise.
- Then exhale and let the book go down.

Belly Breathing starts the feeling of a correct breath while keeping the rest of the body silent, like the shoulders.

Belly Breathing and Exhalation/Support Exercises

- Do the same as above but after you inhale and watch the book rise, immediately count out loud making sure the book doesn't go down.
- Then you can let the book go down by relaxing the abs, but not pulling in.
- Start the process over again.

How many counts are optional. Start with three if that is comfortable. Only do this a few times, maybe at the beginning and the end of the day. You want it to become a natural habit. When you are counting, that would be when you would be singing. When you are doing the exercise and keeping the book up, keep that in mind.

"S"

- After talking in air with teeth apart, smile and put your teeth together but keep your lips apart.
- Let air pass through your front teeth steadily and with force while making an "S" sound.
- After you've done this a few times, then while you're letting the air out, put your hand just above your belly button and just below where your rib cage meets in the front. (The

epigastric area). You should feel an outward tension. Feel this outwardness all around your midsection.

- Next put your hand on your back just above your waist and close to the side. As you let the air out, you should feel an outward tension in the ribs and just below too.
- Keep the "S" sound going for four beats (approx. 4 seconds) and maintain the outwardness you feel throughout your counting. This is how it feels when you exhale and support what you're singing. And yes, this is the same if you are speaking. You always support whether speaking or singing.

"Fist"

- Making a fist with both hands put one in front midway between the belly button and the end of the sternum, and put the other on the side of your body feeling the ribs.
- As you take air in, you will see and feel your hands coming out, now stay out as you hold a note.

You can also have someone put their fist in this area as you sing and speak. As you are singing or speaking, you are pressing against the fist, not away from it. The area is to stay outward. The other person is pressing into you, as you are pressing out to their fist. This causes you to support and allow the air to leave slowly. Caution! Don't pull down.

Remember: When you exhale, singing or speaking, your posture shouldn't deflate, just your lungs. Your skeletal frame should maintain standing up straight. The ribs will go down slowly which should be hardly noticeable, but not your whole frame.

The muscles of inhalation are attached in the front, back, and sides of the body, so it is a *gentle pushing out all the way around* you expand to and hold for breath usage and support.

"Hey"

The "s" exercise can be done slightly different, and instead of "s," you do the exercise with "Hey."

- After taking a small amount of air in, with teeth apart not together, start to say "Hey" on a fairly high and loud note.
- Again you should feel an outward tension all the way around your midsection.
- Keep the chest up.

Summary

- Inhale.
- Muscles are brought into tension.
- Stay expanded & outward as you sing or speak.
- Muscles stay tensed (not overly tensed).
- Air leaves the body slowly and supports your sound.
- RELAX – Return to rest position – muscles relax before you take the next breath. Air can't travel with a tensed muscle. If you see yourself having to raise the chest to get the next breath, you probably didn't relax the abdominal muscles, or your old habit wants to stay with you and you have to work at changing it.
- "KK"- (know that you know) whether you are doing these things correctly by *using a mirror*. I can't stress this enough.

Vocal Anatomy

Where are your lungs? You would be surprised at how many people don't know where the lungs are. Everyone and their brother (or sister) that sings has heard of "sing from the diaphragm." The problem is, too many don't know where or how it works. It just sounds good to say, mostly. The diaphragm is mid pectoral or mid bust, and being the floor of the lungs, they, the lungs, are above.

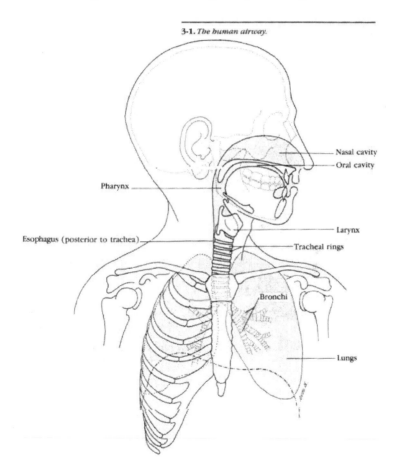

3-1. *The human airway.*

Nasal cavity

Oral cavity

Pharynx

Larynx

Esophagus (posterior to trachea)

Tracheal rings

Bronchi

Lungs

Image from "Anatomical and Physiological Bases of Speech" by David R. Dickson and Wilma M. Dickson and used with their permission

The *thyroid cartilage* is located in the neck and commonly referred to as the *Adam's apple*. The vocal folds reside in back of the thyroid cartilage and are like a "v" lying down, open in the back and attached in the front, and they are actually ligaments. In the back of them is the *arytenoid cartilage* and underneath but open in the center is the *cricoid cartilage;* it looks like a ring. When you are breathing the vocal folds are open, and when you make sound, they are together. The higher you go the longer and thinner they are, and the lower you go they are smaller and thicker. The space between them is called the *glottis*.

4-11. *Laryngeal cartilages, midsagittal section.*

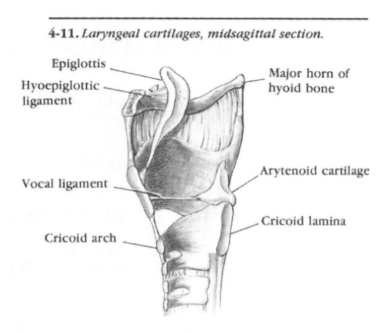

Epiglottis

Hyoepiglottic ligament

Major horn of hyoid bone

Vocal ligament

Arytenoid cartilage

Cricoid lamina

Cricoid arch

Image from "Anatomical and Physiological Bases of Speech" by David R. Dickson and Wilma M. Dickson and used with their permission.

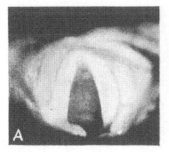
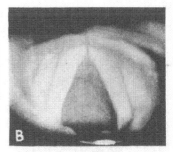

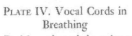

PLATE IV. Vocal Cords in Breathing
A. Position of cords in quiet respiration
B. Breathing in moderate effort
C. Breathing in extreme exertion

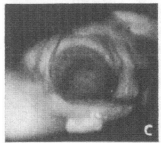

(Bell Telephone Laboratories)

Image from "Keep Your Voice Healthy" by Friedrich S. Brodnitz and reused by permission from Nokia Corporation

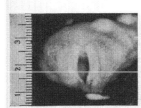
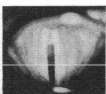
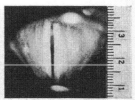

(Bell Telephone Laboratories)

PLATE II. Elongation of Vocal Cords
The photographs represent three stages of stretching of the vocal cords in singing (left to right) a B, b and e¹. The marginal scales do not indicate actual size in inches; they are added to permit comparison of length of vocal cords at various pitches.

Image from "Keep Your Voice Healthy" by Friedrich S. Brodnitz and reused by permission from Nokia Corporation

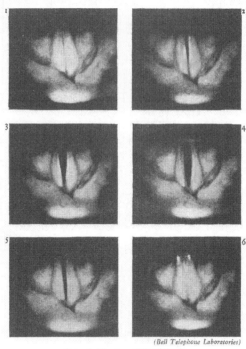

(Bell Telephone Laboratories)

PLATE I. Vibration of Vocal Cords
The photographs show six stages of one full cycle of vibration of the
cords while singing c³.

Image from "Keep Your Voice Healthy" by Friedrich S. Brodnitz
and reused by permission from Nokia Corporation

Opening the Back of the Throat

Thinking of breathing and doing everything right there, is only part of the picture. For support, you must also think of the back of the mouth, the *Uvula*. In back of that is the pharyngeal area which you want to think of keeping wide open, especially when it gets hard to execute difficult notes. One thought is of an umbrella opening up and expanding to the pharyngeal wall. Another helpful thought is yawning. Think of the back of the throat and try to imitate yawning when going for hard and high notes or phrases. You want to lift the soft palate but not drop the jaw too much. This has to accompany the extra outward movement in the abdominal area, as well as keeping the rib cage expanded. It won't matter what you do in the abdominal area if you choke off the sound in the throat though. In fact if you have the outward pressure even moderately correct, it isn't as important as the throat area when it comes to really difficult high notes or passages. Most important is the thought of keeping open, making room so that your sound can come out without encumbrance. Look in a mirror so you don't drop the jaw too far down. You want a fairly wide mouth but not too long. Think of expanding from the front to the back, just under the jaw. Yes, this isn't explaining in medical terms here, but we are trying to open up to sing, so using simple ideas and imagination is way more helpful to the layperson and voice user.

Whenever I have a student trying to get a note, and they are collapsing the throat in some way, I use the term tubing for where the sound travels. They can't close in on it. They try again and get the note. It is imagination, visualization and it works. Here's how it goes.

Tubing

The way sound enters and leaves the body is through tubing, so to speak. Think of the lips as the beginning of your tubing when you inhale, and the end of your tubing as the sound leaves the body. The tubing, starting with the lips, turns downward in the back of the mouth into the throat, neck (*trachea*), and finally the *bronchi,* where it spreads into smaller tubes leading to the *lungs.* It then leaves the lungs and travels back up through the bronchi and trachea to the *vocal folds.* Once it passes the vocal folds, it is sound. Your air (now sound) keeps traveling past the back of the throat to the mouth and lips and then leaves the body. This tubing needs to be rigidly open so as not to constrict the air and sound from flowing in and out, or getting caught or stopped. I have called this your tubing, but I will add something a little different with my imaginary tubing.

> *"Always have a vivid imagination, for you never*
> *know when you might need it." - J.K. Rowling*

What Can We Imagine As Your Tubing? You want to choose a rigid material that you can visualize. It can be plastic - white, black, clear, or any other color. Or it can be metal - silver, gold, bronze, etc. In any case, whether plastic or metal, it is not possible to squeeze in plastic or metal tubing and make it collapse. It is rigid, thus open, which is why we are imagining this. The tubing will have to be around ¾ inches or a little wider in diameter. In the back of the throat it will be an elbow piece but still made of the same material as the rest of the tubing, and again, most of all, these materials are rigidly open. Now imagine taking in air and the air passing through this tube, then the air coming back up and passed the vocal folds, becoming sound and continuing up to the back of your throat. It now goes around the ears, to make sure you are projecting the sound coming out high and off the roof of the mouth. It finishes its journey out past the teeth which can't be closed (tubing, remember?) and finally the lips. You cannot close or collapse this tubing, so the air and sound have no restriction. Start visualizing!

I want to again mention thinking of opening horizontally, (front to back) in the throat just under the chin. The idea of tubing has been very helpful for many students.

Registration

There is much talk on this, and I will add a few words, saying that coordination and balancing of the registers no matter how many you say there are is uppermost. I believe there are two pillars of sound you cannot deny in voice: Chest Voice (registration) and Head Voice (registration) as they are commonly referred to. In men, the same registration called Head Voice is called Falsetto. Chest Voice got its name because you can feel the vibration of sound in the chest when singing in this registration, hence the name. The same is true of Head Voice or Falsetto, which gives the feeling that it is coming from the head. *Dr. Friedrich S. Brodnitz wrote the book "Keep Your Voice Healthy,"* and dedicated it to Manuel Garcia who was a singer, teacher, and scientist that lived from 1805 to 1906. He invented the laryngeal mirror that ear, nose and throat doctors, ENT's used to look down your throat to see the vocal folds. Brodnitz noted that Manuel Garcia was the first to look at vocal folds of a living human; he looked at his own. After the invention of this mirror it was realized that sound comes from the vocal folds and not the chest or head as initially thought. The names have remained. Chest Voice (registration) is also referred to as the low registration and is in charge of the low notes and loud parts of the majority of your sound. Head (Falsetto) Voice (registration) is also referred to as the high registration and is in charge of the higher notes and the softer parts of the majority of your sound. As you are in the area each is in charge of, that registration is dominant. So if you sing a note relatively loud and low you probably will be in Chest Voice. If you sing a note that is fairly high and soft, it probably will be in the Head or Falsetto. Chest Voice gives body, fullness, and luster to the voice while the Head/Falsetto gives height, brilliance, and length. There is a third Registration for females called the Whistle Stop. It is at the highest of the notes in the female voice. In the middle of the vocal range of men is where there are different names given to the sound, such as Head or Mix Registration. Once you identify these different sounds, it doesn't matter what name you put as long as you know how to produce them. Then you will be able to work with whatever name is given. The sound is coming from the same source, your vocal folds, with different areas dominant and different configurations of the vocal folds to make the sounds.

Registration Problems

Middle Breaking

If you started singing at a low note and slid up to higher notes, singing moderately loud, at some point you will break into the Head or Falsetto Voice. At this point, the muscles start to feel stressed and suddenly shift, sometimes a very embarrassingly noticeable shift, to this lighter sound (registration). Hopefully, you are home practicing if this occurs. You needed to get considerably louder to maintain that Chest Voice, (registration). You needed to *cross over the bridge*. Another approach is you needed to lighten up earlier because you are going very high, too high to be able to keep Chest Voice.

Cross Over the Bridge

If you hold a pencil at both ends and bend it, it will break in the middle, which is where your voice will break if you don't make some changes in approaching this area. Decide if you need to go into Head or Falsetto because the range of sound you're going for is very high. Lighten up earlier so that there is a smooth transition. If you are going for Chest, you need to get considerably louder or intense to maintain that sound. Otherwise, your muscles will default to Head or Falsetto.

Chest or Mix With Head

As you go higher in full voice, (Chest) there comes a point where the dominant registration changes from what you are in (Chest) to Head or Falsetto. Before that point, you need to adjust your sound so that you can carry a different, fuller sound which is Chest, into these higher notes. Now the fuller sound which I'm calling Chest is mixed with Head or Falsetto. The dominant registration in the higher notes, which is Head or Falsetto, is the foundation for being able to bring your Chest Voice up to these notes. There are two things that have to happen. The Head or Falsetto has to be strong enough to withstand this extra usage, and the sound has to have more of the qualities of this registration, to execute the sound. It will be a brighter sound. Probably if you are used to singing low, it will feel like it is too bright and it will feel like there is no bottom - like it could fall apart. When it is right you won't feel anything but the sound flying out. Yea!

Private Lessons

If you want to be a pro, you take private lessons - period! You have to stop singing with the artists and be the singer. Be the artist. You need to hear what you sound like and sing it slightly different at specific areas in the song, or completely change it to do your version of the song. Make it your own.

> *If you want to be a pro, you take private lessons - period!*

Classical training is so beneficial as it strengthens your muscles, and can help with all your vocal needs. But you also need more or different training if you are to do other types of music. I use a lot of exercises that are used in classical training, but I also do exercises that classical training would never use and are crucial especially for female singers. Practice with classical lessons for girls is sing chest voice up to a point, and then head voice from there on. Guys would be different as they would more than not, sing in chest voice, but then again would default to Falsetto when the notes are too high. They would be expected to bring the Chest as high as possible but not females. With females you never bring Chest up higher than G above middle C, but in other training you would mix and add Chest to carry that sound higher. This is still called Chest as said before, but it is truly a mix of Head and Chest. Head is what holds it together. Whatever sound, voice, or registration you may be referring to, please continue to be aware that these are referring to the same muscles but different areas and formations of these muscles of the vocal folds.

I called some leading people in voice some years ago and asked them about bringing chest voice up into higher notes for females. That wasn't a legitimate sound, is what they said. I asked about Aretha Franklin, Patty LaBelle, and how they sang the higher notes, and it wasn't head voice. They said they just got used to using their voices that way. I thought okay, that's good for me to know and my students to do… Hmmm. Your muscles are ready to do many things that aren't in the rule book for classical training, but are necessary if you are to do any music that demands higher "quote unquote" chest voice sounds with us girls. The choice is yours. If you are just going to do classical pieces, then you need a classical teacher. Otherwise, just know these facts; be open to classical training as well. Find a teacher for the type of singing you are doing.

The Right Teacher for You

How will I know that the teacher is right? Well, your gut will start to tell you if you feel comfortable with that person. They need to answer your questions. If what they say gets you results and they explain things in a way that you understand, then you will start to know. You need someone who is going to push you and require you to be the best you can be, but also listen to you. If they are impatient going over what you need to do or a problem, they aren't right for you. It doesn't matter if they have a name or not, they need to fit your needs and know how to bring out your talents. The proof is in the pudding.

What is the difference between a teacher and a coach? A coach will be concerned with the whole person and not only with the technical training. They will work on performance, attitude, staging, and any other consideration involving their student. A teacher as I had with Marty Lawrence in New York just did exercises with me and no songs, nothing else. He was an excellent teacher. He taught but I coach. Teachers will go over songs also but there is a difference. Some teachers are coaches and some coaches are teachers. Teachers teach material and coaches inspire you in learning the material and motivate you to be your best in all aspects of your art.

Recording

Hearing and Freaking Out

When you record, you will find that your voice will sound different than it sounds just listening to yourself. Your hearing is set up to hear back from another source. When you record, you hear the actual sound that you make. Most of us are at first in denial or horror at what we hear. "That's not me," or "I don't really sound like that," are common statements we all have made upon first realizing just how we sound. There is hope though. You start to get used to your sound and can adjust for the difference. It will take some time and adjustment, so don't be too critical with yourself; work at adjusting to your sound.

Headphones

Your headphones should be adjusted until you can hear the balance of your voice and the music to your satisfaction. Get your headphone setting correct in the beginning. Do not let a producer or anyone else rush you. It is too important.

"Why Didn't I Fix That?"

As you are finishing your recording, make sure you change the things that you don't like. Even though others may say these parts aren't that bad, change them. You will have to live with this going forward. Every time you listen to it you will say, and I quote, "Why didn't I fix that?" It will be too late unless you have unlimited access to a studio, and you can take the time to re-master, which most of us don't or can't do. So if it bugs you, fix it.

Finding a Good Studio and Producer

Finding a good studio and producer is not an easy task. You may know of someone who loves a studio; go and check it out. If you can hear what a producer has done, that will give you some idea of the quality and taste he or she has, and whether it fits your style and attitude. Check what people say if there are reviews. Make sure the producer will listen to you and your ideas, opinions, and decisions.

Preproduction

Before you go into the studio, you have to go over and over your song. The muscles have to get used to what you will do. If you have a studio at your disposal then you can spend all the time you want perfecting your performance. As you sing your song over and over again, different ways to phrase a part can start to reshape how you sing it. Singing it in front of an audience will give you new insight towards your song also.

When Your Voice Isn't There

Some days the voice doesn't cooperate, and you can go on with the session but may have to change what you do or cut it short. There are days when you least expect it, and you are soaring. Take full advantage of this time.

Don't use too much auto-tune for your voice. It should only be used sparingly and after you really can't seem to have the part or note down after many tries.

Remember, you are going to have to sing these songs live and have to be able to hit all the notes you recorded. A lot of performers nowadays aren't able to do that. They are auto-tuned too much and aren't prepared for live performance. You have to consider the key of the song, to be able to do both recording and live. If you think of all the pressure singing live gives, then you may want to take the key down a step to be able to sing it live. Also, if there is a note you are struggling with, and will worry you when you go to perform, then again, you may have to take the key down. In the studio you can do as many takes as you want to get that note, but live - that is it. You have to do it on the spot. Maybe in the studio you got the note and live you bring the key down. It is good to challenge yourself, but wise to know when you have to consider the whole performance and what will work. Give your best for each show (both in the studio and live).

Music Video

Where Should I Shoot?

We chose the outdoors for my first two videos because I love being outside. Anu Gunn, the producer and director, used old photos to create interest in the first video. The past and present images of me he came up with were a great idea. Everyone that sees it loves it. Make sure you have several different settings to include in your video. What is the song about and where do you love to go?

What Do I Wear?

You can have several outfits to change your look. The sky's the limit so use your imagination for your videos and have fun.

Check the Footage

As you are shooting, in the beginning and throughout, you need to check the footage to see what you like and dislike. This way you can alter how you are standing, walking, and the angle of the body you give to the camera. You want to get great footage so stay on top of things as you shot.

Can You Hear the Track?

Make sure you can hear the track you are syncing to. This avoids a lot of editing and retakes which are expensive. It is only courteous to make sure you have practiced your mouth movements with the track. When I did my first music video I couldn't hear the music I was syncing up to. I thought I just needed to work with it. I needed to say something, and get to where I could hear the track. Anu Gunn and Van Kassabian, who did a lot of editing, had a lot more work to do because of this. Sorry guys. It didn't happen in the next video.

One of Anu's tips is to take your glasses off 15 minutes before taping so the marks from your glasses can leave your face. Practical advice and very helpful.

Wisdom

Before and After a Performance

Before and after you perform you may need to rest. Some performances aren't as demanding as others, but some performances can end with your voice really tired or even damaged. If you consider that the muscles for singing are the same muscles you use for speaking, you will keep your voice quiet before and after you perform. If you are singing and there was no demand, then of course there is no need to rest. Before a performance that is demanding, you may want to keep those muscles quiet the day before and the day of performing or at least be very conscious of your usage. You want them to be optimal when you perform. You still have to warm up though.

If you pushed or if you sang for a long time, and if the performance placed any toll on your voice, then you need to stop and consider the consequence of going out to a party, or doing a lot of talking after the performance.

- The best rest for the voice is sleeping.
- After that is lying down and not talking.
- Next would be relaxing comfortably but no talking.
- Finally, just no talking while you go about your business. Carry a notepad with you and write down what you want to say.

Warming Up

Long show - then your warm up should be shorter but still enough to have your muscles ready. You need to be sure the show line up of songs is suited for your voice to respond the best. If you have difficult songs, don't put them first.

Short show – you need to warm up longer. When I did 5k and 10k runs, our coach, Dr. King Rollins, would have us warm up for 1½ miles. Most of the other runners were sprinting around, but we did a steady 1½ miles, 2 minutes slower than our race time. All of us went home as age group winners. We warmed up those muscles, and you need to warm up your vocal muscles. You may think it will be too much to warm up for 45 minutes, but if the show is short and you need to come out guns blazing, then you need to be ready when you hit the stage!

After a Lot of Singing

Cool Down

Darrel Ebbers, Associate Professor of Voice at the University of the Pacific in California, mentioned in an article published by CD Baby that your voice needs to cool down after singing. Just like any other sport, the voice needs some stretching and light exercises to relax the muscles.

> *Just like any other sport, the voice needs some stretching and light exercises to relax the muscles ...*

- Take a note a little high, and smoothly bring it down lower, see how the voice responds. Sing softly but clear. Do this several times on different but high notes.
- Take a breath in through the nose and exhale through the mouth several times thinking of calming the muscles.
- Air is a lubricant so as you are exhaling, think of the vocal folds relaxing as the air is passing.
- Do the non-vocal exercises, especially the stretch into a yawn.

Rest and Repair

When you use your voice repeatedly, it will need rest. If you worked hard with your voice, there comes the moment you realize you worked your muscles to the bone, and you need to stop and give them time to recoup. Your muscles need to regain their strength.

Remember:

- Sleep is the best if you can manage it.
- Lying down is next.
- Sitting is after that.
- Also, stop talking for short periods of time, and do breathing with thoughts of air passing the vocal folds and soothing them.

If you have damaged your voice, you will need to take more drastic measures to heal. The voice is very resilient so don't panic, just take better care of your instrument. If this is so, you have been depositing into depletion, injury, or abuse. Now it's time you open a new account called restore. The more deposits you make, you tip the scales from bad to good and from injury to healing. You must stop talking. This may feel and be very drastic, but you want to heal your voice. So keep your mouth closed and let it heal. Learn to carry a pad or use your texting skills to talk.

Sometimes you have to talk for parts of the day, so take hours out of each day and don't speak. It may seem impossible but if you want your voice, then you will do it. Your voice will thank you by repairing quickly. Slowly you need to do exercises that re-teach your vocal folds to come together correctly. These exercises should start with a slight "h," so that the vocal folds gently approximate into sound with a vowel following. Go over the Chapter for Voice Therapy as you will need to check your speaking voice as well.

Fight Discontentment

Fight hard for what you want to achieve but also fight hard against discontentment when you cannot get it today. Bring happiness and joy into your life no matter if you have reached your goals or not, but never give up when it is a goal that is worthy of your efforts.

Always look for the Silver Lining

Spiritual

*"It is easy to be independent when you have money.
But to be independent when you haven't got a
thing – that's the Lord's test" – Mahalia Jackson*

There comes a time in every life when we need the strength to overcome a difficulty that comes along. It is going to happen, trust me; it is just part of living. Whatever your belief, you need a source as well as yourself to get you through it. Where do you receive your strength and how do you maintain it? The importance of having a spiritual side is that it gives balance, guidance, and stability to our lives. This doesn't take the place of practice, performing, physical endurance, acting, and learning.

If you watch ball games, you see the players lift their hands or bow their heads in thanksgiving. That usually means that before the game or during, they asked for God's help. The most significant turning point in my life was at 33 when I gave my life to Christ. I said, "God take my life, even my voice. I have made a mess of it. I give it all to you." You may find it foolish or weakness and I respect that. But I strongly suggest you find *your* spiritual source.

When I had to face the fact that I may never sing again from my vocal folds being nicked by doctors, I had to find the strength to go on. It was in prayer with God, my spiritual source and having the guts to tough it out - no giving in. I would go into my prayer closet and then make a phone call to creditors, then back to praying. I did this every few minutes, then every half hour, and then every few hours. Each time I was given the strength to do a little more and I took that strength and used it. So don't forget your spiritual side as well as mental and physical to be well balanced for what comes your way.

> *"I've missed more than 9000 shots in my career.*
> *I've lost almost 300 games; 26 times, I've been*
> *trusted to take the game-winning shot and missed.*
> *I've failed over and over again in my life. And*
> *that is why I succeed."* – Michael Jordan

My life has been imperfect. Predictions about my "making it" haven't happened – yet. I have made lots of mistakes. And then again I have kept going, kept singing, continued learning, kept laughing and living. Through my successes and failures, I encourage you through yours to let you know... It's all good.

Thank you for walking through this journey with me. How insignificant we sometimes feel. Who would care about our stories? But each of our stories is of importance. You matter and what you have to give means much more than you realize. If my sharing causes you to understand that a life so few know can be or make a difference, then I am so happy I opened up, got brave and wrote to you.

Do not grow weary!

REFERENCES

Books

Friedrich S. Brodnitz M.D.: *Keep Your Voice Healthy* – Charles C. Thomas 1953. Associate Attending Otolaryngologist Mount Sinai Hospital, N.Y. City - Adjunct Professor of Communication Sciences, The Institute of Health Sciences Hunter College, The City University of New York

Brendon Burchard: *The Millionaire Messenger* – Free Press 2011 - Founder of Experts Academy

Norman Vincent Peale: *Positive Imaging -The Powerful Way to Change Your Life* - Ballantine Books 1982

Douglas Stanley M.S., Mus.D.: *The Science of Voice* –Carl Fischer 1958

David Ross Dickson, Wilma M. Maue: *Human Vocal Anatomy* – Charles C. Thomas 1970 –

David Ross Dickson, Ph.D. Associate Professor of Anatomy - Associate Professor of Speech University of Pittsburgh, Pittsburgh, Pennsylvania

Wilma M. Maue, M.A. Assistant Director Biocommunications Laboratory University of Pittsburgh, Pittsburgh, Pennsylvania

David Ross Dickson, Ph.D., and Wilma Maue-Dickson, Ph.D.: *Anatomical and Physiological Bases of Speech* – Butterworth-Heinemann 1982

Eugene Feuchtinger: *Your Voice -Methods for strengthening and Developing The Voice* – Nelson-Hall Co., 1953 - A.M. Director, Prefect Voice Institute

Regnier Winsel: *The Anatomy of Voice* – Exposition Press 1966

Enrico Caruso and Luisa Tetrazzini: *Caruso and Tetrazzini on the Art of Singing* – Dover Publications 1975

George A. Brouillet, D.M.D.: *Voice Manual* – Crescendo Publishing Co. 1936

Michael m. Paparella M.d. and Donald A. Shumrick, M.D.: *Otolaryngology – Vol 1* – W.B. Saunders Co. 1973

Michael M. Paparella, M.D. Chairman, Depart. of Otolaryngology The University of Minnesota

Donald A. Shumrick, M.D. Chairman, Depart. of Otolaryngology and Maxillofacial Surgery University of Cincinnati

William Vennard, A.B., B.Music, M.Music: *Singing the Mechanism and the Technic* – Carl Fisher, Inc. 1967- William Vennard - Chairman, Voice Dept. School of Music USC. - Past President, National Ass. of Teachers of Singing

Brene Brown, Ph.D., L.M.S.W: *The Gifts of Imperfection* – Hazelden 2010

Darren Hardy: *The Compound Effect* – Da Capo Press 2010 -Success Mentor to CEO's & high achievers

Tim Grover: *Relentless* – Scribner 2013 – CEO of Attack Athletics

Antiga, Paul Bjorklund, Cecil Carle, Liane Cordes, Paula Culp, Emilio DeGrazia, Karen Casey Elliott, Jeanne Englemann, Patricia Hoolihan, Bonnie-Jean Kimball, Joe Klaas, Roseann Lloyd, Peter McDonald, Beth Milligan, Ann Monson, Pat O'Donnell, and Cynthia Orange: Contributing writers: *Today's Gift*- Hazelden- 1985

Articles

Darrel Ebbers Associate Professor of Voice at the University of the Pacific, in California – CD Baby

Broadcast

Ken Rutkowski: *Business Rockstars*

STUDENTS REVIEWS

"She believed in me, and pushed me ... She's incredible! And so much more than a voice coach ...a life coach, a mentor, and a friend." -Dustin C.

"As a voice teacher, Marquita has helped me with my singing technique, and to strengthen my voice through her own unique exercises and breathing techniques. She is amazing at helping people realize their potential and she is the best cheerleader to have around. …Through Marquita's vocal skills, patience, and encouragement, she helped me to correct my speaking voice, and put an end to any hoarseness." -Susan C.

"Marquita teaches the singer how to put on a performance and captivate the audience's attention." -Aram B.

"Being an awkward teenager with anxieties for singing, I appreciated how she pushed me out of my comfort zone.
…She also teaches you about stage presence and to not be afraid to belt. She helps you gain more range. She works with clients of all ages and helps her clients grow through her encouragement and dedication." -Janine I.

"I have been struggling with vocal nodes. Marquita is helping me to heal without surgery and get through gigs without doing further damage. She is a coach, a healer and also a life guide. I completely trust her with my voice." -Teri G.

"As a child, my family and I suffered from a low income, my parents separated, and my mother was diagnosed with Thyroid Cancer. Through these dark times, Marquita Waters helped me get through with her understanding and caring ways. She taught me to stay optimistic and move forward with life. I recommend Marquita Waters for she was not just an inspirational vocalist, but an appreciated mentor." -Galo L.

"There is nothing like being educated by a true professional that can practice what she preaches and show you how it is done." - Melody A.

"Marquita is a veteran and I was surprised at her range of knowledge. She's sensitive and caring and can belt out a tune like nobody's business. She helped me become a confident speaker again. I will never forget her lessons." -Alison P.

"I have a child that loves going to Marquita because of her smile and jokes which are interwoven between the disciplined lessons and attention to detail." -Paul A.

"Marquita came to my rescue when I had lost my voice completely – with a big concert just several days away.
...To my great surprise and immense gratitude, I was able to give a performance that was called 'flawless' by my producer at the time.
... My voice was restored, through Marquita's wisdom and help. Marquita is a woman of high professional ethics and standards who is uniquely gifted to bring out the very best in her students.
...A thorough knowledge of craft, a wealth of performing experience, and a kind, encouraging way makes Marquita an exceptional teacher of the fine art of singing." -Deirdre R.

"She's not only very experienced in singing and composing music, but she is also quite patient, informative, and helpful as a vocal coach. She finds out exactly where you're at vocally and what needs improvement. She has an extremely well trained ear." -Tiffany H.

"I call her my musical mother because that is how much she cares about each of her students." -Yesenia G.

"Marquita is a great teacher with an amazing energy and presence that quickly makes you feel comfortable. Before the end of the lesson I was hitting notes I didn't know I could hit." -Brandon J.

"She will be tough on you but it pays off at the end! She will support you and help you in whatever you're going through. Be ready to explore new things and have fun." - Erika E.

"If you are passionate about singing and want to improve no matter if you are a beginner or expert, Marquita is a great choice." -Chris M.

ABOUT THE AUTHOR

Marquita Waters is a multifaceted performing artist based out of Los Angeles, California. She was represented by The William Morris Agency and released music as the critically acclaimed Mia Morrell during the Frank Sinatra era. She has appeared on *The Tonight Show with Johnny Carson*, *The Merv Griffin Show* and *The Steve Allen Show*. Her voice can be heard on the hit TV Show, *The Nanny* and the trailer of the Blockbuster film, *Ghostbusters II*.

Marquita continues to release music as an independent artist. She has released Contemporary Christian singles such as "I Will Not Grow Weary," "Just About Lovin' You Lord," and "Christ," a swing album titled, "Gotta Get It Right" and a walk cassette called, "Walking With God." She also has been a Vocal Coach for 30 years and is still coaching to this day.

Marquita was a competitive runner for 20 years. She has completed several Marathons finishing in the top 300 women and is an All-American in 5K and 10K races. She spent seven years ministering at a minimum security camp for boys who were felons and has devoted many years to rescuing dogs and cats… and they still seem to know her address.

MARQUITA WATERS
(FKA MIA MORRELL)
DISCOGRAPHY

MIA MORRELL
Side A: "Ci Vediamo (I'll Be Seeing You)"
Side B: "Everytime I See You"
United Artists – 45 RPM vinyl single – December 1966

Side A: "I Have A Mind Of My Own"
Side B: "Sunshine And Roses"
ABC Records – 45 RPM vinyl single – July 1967

Side A: "Special People"
Side B: "Who Are You"
ABC Records – 45 RPM vinyl single – September 1967

MARQUITA WATERS
"Walking With God"
Running Song Music – Cassette – 1993

MARQUITA WATERS
"Gotta Get It Right"
Running Song Music – MP3 & CD Album – August 4, 2006

MARQUITA WATERS
"I Will Not Grow Weary (Faithful and True)"
MP3 Single – October 27, 2014

"Christ"
MP3 Single – June 14, 2017

"Loving You Lord"
MP3 Single – Coming Soon
Running Song Music

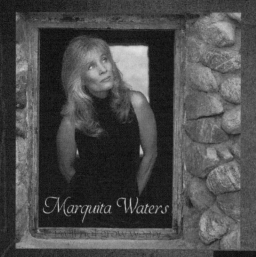

Marquita Waters

LOVING YOU LORD

MARQUITA WATERS

CHRIST

MARQUITA WATERS

Writing this book brought back many memories. All the work to bring it to life was a journey that strengthened and confirmed the fact that I will not grow weary.

Made in the USA
Las Vegas, NV
23 May 2023

72472212R00122